THE
CHINESE MYTHS

THE
CHINESE MYTHS
A GUIDE TO THE
GODS AND LEGENDS

TAO TAO LIU

To CT, who helped me at the end when I was ill

A NOTE ON ROMANIZATION

Many early books on China used a confusing variety of transliteration systems.
In 1958 the Chinese government imposed the *Hanyu Pinyin*
('the Chinese language as spoken by the Chinese made into spelled sounds'),
which became the official standard for all Romanized spellings in Chinese.
Pinyin also became the basis for the teaching of the Chinese language in China.
This is the system followed in this book.

HALF-TITLE Roof tile fragment with dragon, probably Ming dynasty.

FRONTISPIECE A Ming-dynasty hanging scroll painting of Fu, Lu and Shu:
the Daoist gods of Fortune, Prosperity and Longevity.

First published in the United Kingdom in 2022 by
Thames & Hudson Ltd, 181A High Holborn, London WC1V 7QX

First published in the United States of America in 2022 by
Thames & Hudson Inc., 500 Fifth Avenue, New York, New York 10110

Reprinted 2024

The Chinese Myths © 2022 Thames & Hudson Ltd, London

Text © 2022 Tao Tao Liu

British Library Cataloguing-in-Publication Data
A catalogue record for this book is available from the British Library

Library of Congress Control Number 2022931900

ISBN 978-0-500-25238-3

Printed and bound in Slovenia by DZS-Grafik d.o.o.

CONTENTS

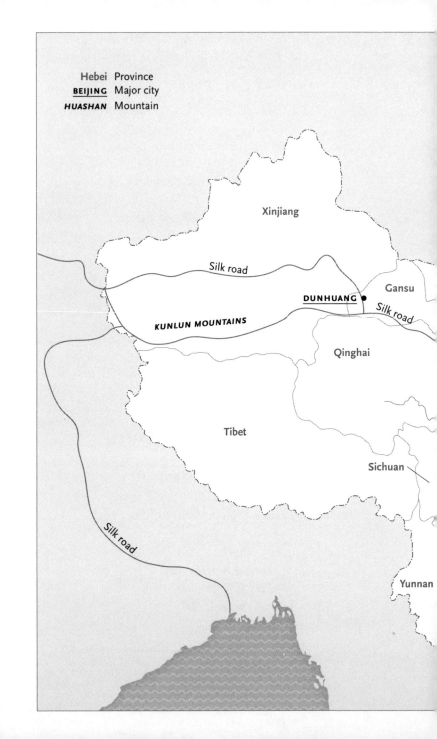

Hebei Province
BEIJING Major city
HUASHAN Mountain

Xinjiang

Silk road

DUNHUANG ● Gansu

Silk road

KUNLUN MOUNTAINS

Qinghai

Tibet

Sichuan

Silk road

Yunnan

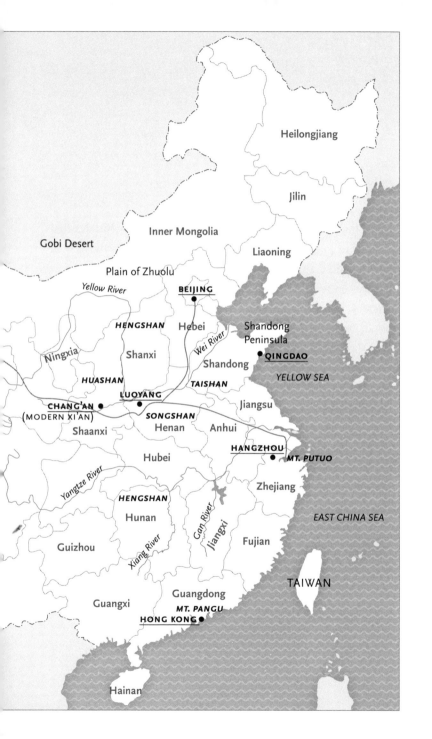

1

A BRIEF HISTORY OF
CHINESE MYTHOLOGY

More than two thousand years ago, the Chinese told tales that rivalled in complexity the ones told almost contemporaneously in Greece. These legends speak to the core beliefs and concerns of an agrarian society based on the banks of the ever-shifting Yellow River. We meet heroes like Gun and Yu, who buttressed the land against floods on the scale of the biblical inundation, and Yi the Archer, who shot down nine of the ten suns that existed when the world was new, fending off wildfires and drought. One story tells how the creator goddess, Nuwa, crafted humankind from the yellow clay of the alluvial plain. These ancient stories, passed down over centuries in an age before writing, encapsulate beliefs that were developed in the philosophies of native Daoism and, later, Buddhism, imported from India. Despite this rich tradition, people in the west are far more familiar with the myths that have come down to us from the Greeks and Romans, and know almost nothing of the myths of China.

This is partly to do with the unfamiliarity of China to the western mind; the Chinese imagination has developed quite differently from that of the west over its long history. Even the concept of 'mythology' is fundamentally a western one, foreign to China, where it is translated as *shenhua*, 'words/talk on the subject of gods/deities'. It was introduced only at the beginning of the twentieth century from Europe, via Japan, along with other ideas then developing in the humanities. The word *shenhua* was first used to refer to myths in the manner of the western tradition: stories from ancient times. For the purpose of this book, I take the meaning of *shenhua* to refer largely to the myths of China's 'classical era', found in sources that date mainly to between the sixth century BCE, during the Eastern Zhou dynasty, and the middle of the third century CE, the end of the Han dynasty. We shall also look at the myths of the 'imperial era', which lasted from the reign of Qin Shi Huangdi, first emperor of the Qin dynasty, until the establishment of the Republic of China in 1911. Over this period Chinese religion and beliefs became more fractured and much busier, with a proliferation of myths and gods worshipped for their particular efficacy as different challenges were faced. The Chinese idiom *bao fo jiao*, 'embracing the Buddha's foot', captures this sentiment: it is used to satirize people who do not express devotion to the Buddha until their hour of need.

Many of the mythological figures of the imperial era developed out of historical persons, and the importance of history is characteristic of this more recent mythology. For example, the genial general and military hero of the Three Kingdoms period, Guan Yu, was declared the God of War by the Wanli emperor of the Ming in 1594 in a mythicization of history. The annual Dragon Boat Festival held in the fifth month of the lunar calendar involves ceremonies placating the dragon gods of China's rivers as well as commemorating the upright official Qu Yuan of the Eastern Zhou period, who drowned himself in despair over his failure to influence a bad ruler.

Unlike the Greco-Roman myths, which have been shaped into canonical narratives by writers such as Homer, Hesiod and Ovid, those from China tend to be laconic, often appearing in contradictory arrangements that speak of different traditions. Many of the

The National Minorities

When we speak of 'the Chinese', we tend to mean the Han people. The Han were but one of many groups that lived in the area that we now call China in the first millennium BCE, and through military conquest came to dominate the land. Today they account for more than 95 per cent of the population, but there are fifty-five non-Han ethnic groups in China, numbering millions of people.

The Han culture was the most technologically advanced, and borrowed from many neighbouring peoples, a trait still true now. The Han dynasty (202 BCE–220 CE) has come to be thought of as the beginning of the 'high culture' of China. Yet the Han writers drew on the myths of other ethnic groups, including, notably, those of the Miao and Yao people; these myths have changed little even over millennia, owing to their reliance on oral traditions (see p. 37).

modern ethnic groups in China, such as the Miao, kept their strong oral traditions, either not having a written script or being less reliant on one. It is generally accepted now that tribal myths and legends had a part to play in the development of Chinese mythology, and nowadays we find that many myths among the so-called minorities, collected in the recent past, still bear a striking resemblance to the main myths of the Han dynasty.

It was only in the twentieth century that scholars first attempted a critical analysis of the *shenhua* of the classical era. Up to then, writers and historians had collected and preserved the ancient texts, building a corpus of authentic, original sources, but had not rigorously examined them, and indeed had often edited them to better align with the principles of Confucius' philosophy (see p. 20). But since the establishment of the Republic of China in 1911, folklorists such as Gu Jiegang (1893–1980), one of the founders of the *Yigupai* ('Doubting Antiquity School'), have challenged the accounts of the Confucianist elite.

THE PLACE OF MYTH IN DAILY LIFE

The great myths of the classical era may preoccupy scholars, but the accumulation of myth and legend over thousands of years can be seen in the abundance of temples and places of worship throughout China and the development of annual cycles of ritual and observance, some followed countrywide, some strictly local. It was estimated that in Beijing alone between 1400 and 1900 there were some 2,500 temples, mainly Buddhist but also associated with the imperial cult,

The Hall of Prayer for Good Harvests in the Temple of Heaven complex in Beijing, founded in the first half of the fifteenth century.

A Song-dynasty scroll painting of Yu,
tamer of floods and founder of the Xia dynasty.

Daoism, Confucianism and local cults. They were all full of worshippers on a regular basis, some holding monthly fairs as well as regular festivals. Even in the small town of Shaoxing on the south shore of Hangzhou bay, there are currently thirteen Buddhist temples, one Daoist temple, and one strictly local shrine to a young woman who drowned in 151 CE trying to save her father's life, not to mention the nearby shrine at the tomb of the great Yu, tamer of floods. These represent a small proportion of the temples and shrines that would have existed in previous centuries.

The great Yu, founder of the semi-legendary Xia dynasty (*c.* 2070–1600 BCE), is a figure who achieved divine status for his hydrographic

A thirteenth- or fourteenth-century woodblock print of the warrior god
Guan Yu, deified hero of the *Romance of the Three Kingdoms*.

innovation, which not only saved lives but established the basis of
agriculture through irrigation. He is not only worshipped as divine,
in Shaoxing he also has a tomb, just as any mortal being would. His
tomb was famously visited by the First Emperor, Qin Shi Huangdi, in
210 BCE and a stele (now lost) was erected to commemorate the event.

The most popular deities in Beijing were the warrior god Guandi
and the Buddhist goddess Guanyin. Guandi derived from the historic figure Guan Yu (162–220), famous for his martial achievements
and loyalty during the political turbulence of the end of the Han
dynasty. His role in the conflict was mythologized in the *Romance
of the Three Kingdoms*, one of the Great Classical Novels that is still

celebrated in traditional Chinese entertainments today. Held up for centuries as the pre-eminent martial hero, Guandi was declared a god in the Ming dynasty and his fierce, red-faced image was placed in many temples and shrines as a protection against evil spirits. He epitomizes the Chinese habit of deifying 'real' people, demonstrating the primary importance of history in the creation of mythology in the early imperial period.

The compassionate Bodhisattva Guanyin, whose full name means 'the one who sees and heeds the cries of the world', was an Indian Buddhist icon whose appearance and significance were transformed in China. Originally a male deity, depicted in Tang paintings from

Guanyin, goddess of compassion, who was
adopted from Indian Buddhism.

Dunhuang with a thin moustache and beard, Guanyin gradually acquired more female attributes in China and was associated with salvation and the provision of children. In Ming-dynasty porcelain figurines, Guanyin has lost the moustache and often carries a small child in 'her' arms. She appears female although she is never depicted with the bound feet suffered by many (usually upper and middle class) Chinese women from the twelfth century onwards. The image of Guanyin is universal in Buddhist temples and is worshipped particularly by those desiring children.

THE ANNUAL CYCLE

There are fixed points in the lunar calendar, established by the Western Han Emperor Wu (r. 141–87 BCE), when people all over China share rituals in honour of particular deities or beliefs. China being originally an agrarian society, the main events occur in winter, when farming communities would have downed tools, but by the Han dynasty were sufficiently prosperous that agricultural surplus supported communal celebrations. Festivals gave rural populations a rare opportunity to come together, and troupes of actors and storytellers put on performances, undoubtedly the origin of many of the stories that have come down to us.

When the Republic of China adopted the Gregorian calendar in 1911, bringing the country in line with the empires of Europe, the traditional new year celebration became known as the Lunar New Year. It is also sometimes called the Spring Festival, as it coincides with the period in the old agricultural calendar when farmers would start to plough their fields and sow crops after the passing of winter.

On the third day of the first month of the year, Chinese families worship the God of Wealth both at home and in local temples. Caishen, God of Wealth, was said to have helped the Zhou defeat the Yin dynasty riding a black tiger, and was depicted in temples surrounded by attendants. Soon after comes *Yuanxiao*, the Lantern Festival, in which brightly coloured lanterns are carried through the dark streets for people to admire.

Early in the third month, on *Qingming* ('Bright and Clear'), the only festival without a fixed point in the lunar calendar, families go out to sweep, weed, and tidy ancestral graves. They make offerings to their ancestral spirits, sprinkling the graves with wine and laying food in front of them. After the spirits have had their opportunity to partake of the food, the family tuck in and have a picnic in the graveyard. This tradition began during the Song dynasty, when Confucian notions of filial piety became important.

The Buddha's birthday is celebrated on the eighth day of the fourth month, and *Duanwu*, the Dragon Boat Festival, follows on the fifth day of the fifth month. People race boats in the hopes that the dragons of the sky, who bring rain, will also make an appearance – a grave concern in an agricultural society. The fifth month also sees the celebration of Zhong Kui, the demon-slayer whose image is posted on doors to celebrate his destruction of centipedes, scorpions, toads, snakes and lizards. On the seventh of the seventh month is the Festival of the Cowherd and the Weaver Girl, when the two stars Altair and Vega are closest to the Milky Way and the two lovers (the cowherd and the weaver girl, living in the stars) can meet over a bridge formed by a flock of magpies. Traditionally girls float needles in bowls of water to see from the shadow cast whether they will become skilful embroiderers and thus easily find a husband. The fifteenth day of the seventh month is the Festival of Hungry Ghosts, when offerings are made to the dead and paper boats with little lanterns in them are launched onto rivers and lakes to help save the souls of the dead.

On the fifteenth day of the eighth month, when the moon is at its roundest, mooncakes are eaten and given as gifts and debts are settled. This is known as the Mid-Autumn Festival, and is almost as popular as the Lunar New Year, and another occasion on which it is very important for families to come together.

Since the Qing dynasty, a number of public holidays were added to this annual cycle of festivals, usually on the day that matched the number of the month in the lunar calendar; for example, on the ninth day of the ninth month, known as the 'Double Ninth', on which people visit their ancestor's graves or climb hills to eat together and celebrate with chrysanthemum wine. The twelfth month sees preparations for the Lunar New Year, a public holiday lasting three days: houses are cleaned, images of demon-frightening gods pasted on front doors, and special meals prepared. The image of the Stove God in the kitchen is smeared with honey, either so that he will make a sweetly favourable report on the household on his annual visit to heaven, or to glue up his mouth and tongue to prevent him from saying anything that might cause the family ill will. The tradition of sitting up all night, *Shousui* ('Watching the Year Pass'), to greet the New Year is still observed.

Almost all of these celebrations contain a mixture of ancient and more recent mythology, of historical and mythical persons, and strong local variations (see Appendix).

MYTHS OF THE CLASSICAL ERA

Scholars, both Chinese and non-Chinese, of the present and recent past have done sterling work rebuilding the corpus of ancient myths of the classical era, which had been all but lost. Nevertheless, the yield is not large compared with those that have survived from the imperial era, and most of the ancient myths are fragmentary or laconic, so many of our sources refer to them only briefly, in the course of their discussions of other literary or philosophical subjects.

Many early writings no longer survive, since from the later Han, most texts were written on paper, which replaced the more durable bamboo slips of the earlier period. The earliest surviving 'books', also printed on paper, date from the Song. The contents of earlier writings, where the complete text no longer survives, are often known only from references in compilations called *leishu,* which are gatherings of quotations from existing texts often arranged by subject. Compiled from about 300 CE throughout the imperial era, these compendia offer tantalizing references to lost works.

Nowadays China is seen as a unified whole, but during the majority of the Eastern Zhou dynasty (770–256 BCE) it was essentially a confederation of city states. Each of these places would have had their own myths, which remained in circulation for as long as the rise and fall of the states, passed down the generations through the oral tradition. The lesser states were swallowed up by bigger ones until the Qin dynasty imposed its rule on the whole of the country in 221 BCE, thus beginning the imperial era, which lasted two thousand years, right up to the twentieth century.

Classical texts tell us that before the Zhou dynasty, there were the Xia and the Shang dynasties, but it is very difficult to separate fact

The Land

China is almost as large as continental Europe, and like Europe is host to a huge variety of not only languages and customs but also landscapes and climates. In the north lie the arid plains of the Yellow River, with its dry winters and hot summers; in the south, a thousand miles away, it is tropical. High mountains lie in the west, from where the two great rivers, the Yellow River and the Yangtze, flow eastward, discharging into the Yellow Sea and the East China Sea respectively.

from myth in these accounts. Euhemerization, named after the Greek mythographer Euhemerus, is a term for treating myths as ancient Greek history imperfectly remembered. If the Greeks can be said to have mythologized their history, the Chinese historicized their myths. It is to the Han dynasty (202 BCE–220 CE), which bridged both ancient and imperial China, that we look for the earliest of our written sources, as this period saw the rise and flourishing of the literati, or scribal class. The Han-dynasty scholar Sima Qian (c. 145–86 BCE), considered the father of Chinese historiography, started his *Shiji* ('Records of the Grand Historian') with reference to the myths of the Xia and Shang dynasties and attempted to historicize these ancient stories – a typically Confucian habit. Our problem, then, is twofold: we must endeavour to find sources that pre-date the Han, and we must carefully evaluate the extent to which we can trust the Han sources that are more readily available to us.

CONFUCIAN PHILOSOPHY

The politician and philosopher Confucius (551–479 BCE) achieved great and enduring fame because what he said was simple to understand and follow. Confucius was a rationalist, but he was also agnostic, in the twenty-first century sense of the word. Although he did not believe in the gods that were passed down through the oral tradition, he was conscious of a godlike presence, and believed in what he called *tian*, 'heaven'. *Tian* stood for a moral code that must not be broken. It was like the word of God in the Christian way of thought.

Confucius believed that the Western Zhou had handed down the rules of morality. Furthermore, he believed that these rules constituted the ideal society, provided that kings and ministers followed the prevailing ethics of righteousness and benevolence. It was because leaders were not following these rules that the country was falling into decline. During the Spring and Autumn period when Confucius lived, there was a great deal of internecine warfare, with the larger states absorbing the smaller ones. As he saw it, until the country's rulers re-established the moral order and rituals that had existed in the Western Zhou before its demise – which was entirely due to the incompetence or laxity of its later kings – there was no hope for society. He called this the *tianming* ('mandate of heaven') conferred upon a moral ruler, who saw to it that his descendants would abide by the moral code until an immoral ruler 'lost' the mandate of heaven, at which point heaven would once again confer the mandate, starting a new dynasty. Confucius himself gave some encouragement to 'rebels' in his philosophy, provided that the 'rebel' was trying to restore what had been moral and proper before corruption had permeated the land.

大成至聖文宣王

A Yuan-dynasty ink drawing of the philosopher Confucius (551–479 BCE).

Confucius also placed high importance on the values of family and shared ancestry. In modern-day China, honouring ancestors is still important; it is not uncommon to encounter a shrine to the ancestors in family homes, usually placed in a room devoted to them. The festival of *Qingming* ('Bright and Clear'), often called Tomb-Sweeping Day, usually celebrated at the beginning of April, is attended by the whole family to commemorate the lives of departed relatives. Confucius' stress on the virtues of the rulers of the distant past and the importance of conservative rituals did not appeal to the rulers of his time, who were more concerned with the practicalities of interstate warfare.

Unable to persuade any ruler to follow his ideas in his lifetime, the rise of Confucius' popularity was gradual, beginning during the Warring States period in the Eastern Zhou dynasty (476–221 BCE).

The Twenty-four Exemplars of Filial Piety

Part of Confucius' emphasis on the importance of family lay in the concept of filial piety or devotion to parents. A very popular book, probably compiled during the Yuan dynasty, *Ershisi Xiao* ('Twenty-four Exemplars of Filial Piety'), includes stories of gratitude and service to parents. It starts with the story of the legendary Emperor Shun, ill-treated by his step-mother and nearly killed by his father, but nevertheless exhibiting intense filial piety. He was chosen as a worthy successor by Emperor Yao, whose own son was not, in his opinion, good enough to serve. Thus, in Shun's case, filial piety was rewarded. The second exemplar was the Emperor Wen of the Han (r. 180–157 BCE), who cared for his mother during three years of illness. He never undressed so that he would be ready to serve her day and night and personally tasted all of her medicines to make sure they were safe. The other stories are also of 'real' historical persons: Wu Meng, who at the age of eight slept beside his parents' bed so that the mosquitoes would bite him rather than them; Wang Xiang, who lay naked on a frozen pond to catch the carp that his cruel stepmother loved to eat; and Wang Pu, whose mother was very frightened of thunder. After she died, if there was a thunderstorm, he would rush to her tomb to tell her not to be afraid. Other stories include: 'Carrying rice over long distances to feed his parents', 'Selling oneself into servitude to cover father's funeral expenses', 'Playing like a child to amuse elderly parents', 'Breast-feeding (toothless) mother-in-law', 'Cleaning the chamber-pot in person' and 'Tasting faeces causes despair', in which a son was advised to taste his sick father's faeces. If they were bitter-tasting then he was getting better, but they tasted sweet, which was very bad news. Apart from the story of Emperor Shun, in most cases there was no special reward for filial devotion, repaying parents for all they had done and bringing them happiness was enough.

Confucius' influence grew further with the rise of the scribal class in the Han dynasty (202 BCE–220 CE), and his philosophy has remained dominant in China into the twentieth century. It is during the Han dynasty that our records of the ancient myths begin to divide. The written language lay in the hands of the Confucianist elite. The other form of language was the vernacular: the language people actually spoke. Confucius disliked fiction of any kind, even allegorical fiction, preferring history that told the real actions of real people over myths. His interest in history influenced his followers, and so they historicized many myths in the Han dynasty, moulding them to their way of thinking; for instance, turning the mythical figure of the Yellow Emperor (see p. 82) into a true, historic leader.

Confucianism might not have encouraged belief in gods, but did not proscribe their worship; it seems instead to have left such matters to individual consciences. The result was that the common

The Epic of Darkness

In 1982, an old farmer in Shennongjia, Hubei Province, gave the writer Hu Chongjun a rare manuscript recording the oral tradition of the region. Over the following years, Chongjun collected a number of other manuscripts – some incomplete, and each differing in some small way – from Shennongjia, a little-known, thinly populated mountainous area and UNESCO-recognized place of natural beauty; exactly the sort of place where the oral tradition persisted to within living memory. He compiled them into a new edition of the Tang-dynasty *Hei An Zhuan* ('Epic of Darkness'). Because of its length, this tale was seldom performed except at funerals, hence its name. It tells the story of the founding of the world, along with other early myths.

people went on with their temple-building, telling their traditional stories about gods and other divinities and celebrating them in rituals and festivals, while Confucians, at least ostensibly, eschewed them. Since the greater part of the population did not know how to read and write, the tales of gods, ghosts and spirits – divinities of which Confucius would have disapproved – continued to be passed down in the oral tradition.

DAOISM

Daoism, an ancient philosophy peculiar to China, is hard to define. It differs from western religions, which tend to focus on one all-powerful god. Rather, Daoism bases itself on the natural world: it is the numinous; it is the things themselves before humans have got at them; it is like water, which given time will wear down the hardest of materials; it is the Yin and Yang, the opposing forces in every thing. Yang is the masculine principle of light and heat, positive and active, while Yin is the receptive, feminine principle of darkness and the cold. Neither can do without the other, just as shadows can be cast only where there is light.

The Yin and Yang combine with the Five Directions (north, south, east, west and centre) to make all the fundamentals of life. Yang characterizes the south and east – the sun, rising in the east, is referred to as the Great Yang – while Yin characterizes the west and north. The Five Directions, as well as their associated elements and colours, and the seasons were of immense importance in all aspects of life and death in China. Death and disease were associated with the north, from which the north wind brought epidemics, and winter; thus the dead were

Left: An ink drawing of the Lord of the East. *Right:* The God of the Eastern Sky. From a fourteenth-century album of eleven paintings relating to the *Nine Songs*.

interred facing towards the north. Clothes, ornaments, and offerings used in ritual practice had to conform to the appropriate colours. The emperor 'reigns facing the south' to receive the warmth and fresh-ness of the sun, and his subjects face the north while in his presence.

The Five Directions and Five Elements

The number five has great symbolic value in Chinese thought, evoking a cross with its centre and thus expressing universality. Early Chinese mythic texts name five gods who each rule one of the Five Directions and one of the Five Elements (wood, fire, metal, water and earth) that encompass the whole world in traditional Chinese philosophy. According to the *Huainanzi* ('Writings of the Huainan'):

The east is wood. Its god is Taihao. His assistant is
Goumang. Both hold the compasses and govern spring....
The south is fire. Its god is the Flame Emperor [Zhurong].
His assistant is Zhuming. They hold the beams of steelyard
and govern summer.... The centre is earth. Its god is
Huang Di [the Yellow Emperor]. His assistant is Houtu.
They both hold the ropes and govern the four directions....
The west is metal. Its god is Shaohao. His assistant is
Rushou. They hold the carpenters' square and govern
autumn.... The north is water. Its god is Zhuanxu.

Houtu, the Earth God

Houtu is not clearly delineated in any of our sources and does
not have the status traditionally attributed to the 'earth god' in the
mythologies of other cultures. He is mentioned only as the ancestor
of the minor god Kuafu (see p. 57) in the *Shan Hai Jing* ('Classic
of Mountains and Seas'). According to the *Huainanzi*, he assists
Huang Di and thus belongs to the centre. In a later annotation to
the *Chu Ci* ('Songs of Chu'), he was the ruler of the netherworld,
supported by a forbidding assistant called Tubo, who guarded
the entrance.

In later traditions and popular religion Houtu was female, with
many temples dedicated to her. At a temple in Wanrong County,
Shaanxi Province, she is called 'Houtu, the sacred mother' and is
portrayed wearing a crown and a skirt embroidered with phoenixes,
symbols of royalty. Local records indicate that the temple dates back
to the Han dynasty, and was visited by more than ten emperors up
to the Song dynasty. Today pilgrims pray to the goddess for the
usual things: a safe journey on the Yellow River, a good harvest,
rain or children.

His assistant is Xuanming. They hold the weights of steelyards, and govern winter.

The names of the five gods associated with these directions and elements vary in different sources. However, Huang Di ('the Yellow Emperor') and his grandson Zhuanxu are always present. Colours, by association with the elements, are also by extension linked to different directions. The east belongs to wood, so its colour is green; south/fire is red; west/metal is white; north/water is black; and the centre/earth is yellow (appropriately governed by the Yellow Emperor).

LAOZI

Legend tells us that Laozi, a near contemporary of Confucius living in the sixth century BCE, was one of the progenitors of Daoism and author of the great *Daode Jing* ('The Book of the Way and its Virtue'), which sets out of the fundamental philosophy of Daoist thought in poetic metaphors. (Scholars, on the other hand, have long told us that this book was written by many different hands, and some say that Laozi himself in fact lived during the Warring States period, in the fourth century BCE.) 'Laozi' is an honorific title meaning 'old master'; his actual surname is given as Li in various historical accounts. The Han-dynasty historian Sima Qian tells us that, after spending years as a recluse in the countryside, Laozi returned to the city of Luoyang where the gatekeeper, Yin Xi, recognized him as a great scholar and became his disciple. He is worshipped as Taishang Laojun ('the Great Old Lord') and one of the Three Pure Ones of Daoism, and even appears in the Ming-dynasty historical romance

The Three Pure Ones

The first of the Three Pure Ones, or Three Divine Teachers, is Yuanshi Tianzun ('the Original One, Respected of Heaven'), also known as the *Yuqing* ('Jade Pure One'). He was supposed to be the instructor to Laozi, who is himself the third, known as Taishang Laojun or the *Taiqing* ('Extreme Pure One'). The second, known as the *Shangqing* ('Upper Pure One'), is Taishang Daojun ('the Lord of the Dao'), who is supposed to know all that is known about the Dao. Each of these deities ruled over a heaven, and manifested one of the forms of *qi*, or celestial energy. They dominated early Daoist religion, making their presence felt before the appearance of the emperor, who was the highest man in the land, but they probably held these positions before the sorting into high or low was known to the Chinese as a feature of the imperial period.

The Taoist triad.

Xi You Ji ('Journey to the West'; see p. 169) as a member of the court of the Jade Emperor. In that tale he imprisons the famous Monkey, though without doing him any actual harm.

Despite its disputed authorship, the *Daode Jing* is one of the most important books of early Daoism. The other is the *Zhuangzi*, composed in the late Warring States period by Zhuangzi, after whom it was named. Zhuangzi built on Daoist philosophy, often using fragments of contemporary myths to make his point. He seldom tells the whole story when referring to these mythic episodes, presumably because he assumed his readers would already be familiar with them. This is one of the reasons that myths in the written sources come down to us in fragments.

A tenth-century bronze sculpture of the Daoist philosopher Laozi,
also known as Taishang Laojun ('the Great Old Lord').

CHAPTER 1

BUDDHIST INFLUENCES

Buddhism arrived in China in approximately the first century CE, towards the end of the Han dynasty. In response to this new faith, Daoism took on more features of a pantheistic religion. It acknowledged the existence of the *numen*, or spirit, in natural things: animals; inanimate objects, such as trees; and humans. It was with the advent of Buddhism that Daoism became more recognizable as a religion; before, Daoism was simply what was 'supranormal', or supernatural. Yet Daoism proved itself protean, transforming to survive alongside the newly introduced religion. For instance, there had been no hint of monasticism in Daoism until the arrival of Buddhism, after which it began to produce its own brand.

Indeed, Buddhism may have gained its first foothold in China as a variant of Daoism. Many aspects of Buddhism echoed the native religion: they both taught the value of moral acts and meditation on the path to personal salvation. Daoism adapted new, foreign elements introduced by Buddhism to fit with the native tradition so that they became peculiarly Chinese, such as the image of Guanyin, goddess of compassion, which originated in Indian Buddhism (see p. 151). And while the Chinese myths had existed long before Buddhism began to take hold in the country, later it would influence greatly the development of a rich tradition of legends, a different manifestation of the Chinese imagination.

The ancient myths were not forgotten; they were told by ordinary people, passed from generation to generation, and were treated with the same reverence with which Christians regard the stories in the Old Testament of the Bible. And while Buddhists and Daoists built new temples according to their new religious dictates, many

The altar of a Buddhist temple in Shenyang.

temples devoted to the old gods still survive. For instance, there are many shrines dedicated to the popular creator-god Pangu (see p. 50), including one on top of the mountain that bears his name in the Tongbai region of Henan Province, his supposed residence. On the third day of the third month of the lunar calendar, Mount Pangu hosts a huge festival that draws many pilgrims to this temple.

WESTERN PERSPECTIVES

By the time that western missionaries arrived in China, towards the end of the nineteenth century and the beginning of the twentieth, they found themselves in the midst of a huge pantheon of 'popular beliefs', which they duly set down in their journals. To them there seemed to be no limit to the magic inherent in the Chinese worldview.

Missionaries and anthropologists also wrote about their encounters with shamanism. In fact, shamanistic practices give us our earliest evidence of writing in China, on so-called 'oracle bones',

Divination and the Eight Trigrams

The art of predicting the future, or divination, goes back in China at least as far as the Shang dynasty, from which we find some of the earliest examples recorded on the so-called 'oracle bones'. These were ox shoulder bones or turtle or tortoise shells inscribed – using symbols or 'characters' derived from early pictograms – with questions, usually related to the concerns of kings. Once heated, the bone would crack, and the resulting cracks or lines were interpreted by ritual specialists – the *wu* – to divine the answers to the inscribed questions. A text by the Han sceptic philosopher Wang Chong (27–100 CE) gives us one example of an inauspicious divination: 'When King Wu of the Zhou was about to attack King Zhou of the Shang, he had divination using stalks, but the result was negative. The diviner declared, "Very bad luck." The Great Lord pushed aside the stalks and trod on the tortoises, and said, "What do dried bones and dead plants know about fate!"'

Other methods of divination developed and manuals were written to help practitioners recognize the signs. Among these were *bagua* ('the Eight Trigrams') said to have been created by the god which were used in divination ceremonies in the Shang dynasty. The Tungusic word *shaman* was adopted by nineteenth-century anthropologists, and their practices seem to mirror those of the *wu* in ancient China, who acted as healers and oracles, mediators between humans and the divine. In the Shang dynasty, it seems that the *wu* took great offices of state, interpreting the oracle bones that kings relied upon to judge the auspiciousness of their actions (see box below). However, the practice declined in the Zhou dynasty, perhaps owing to greater scepticism on the part of the followers of Confucius. Eventually even the *wu*'s role as healers was greatly

Fuxi (see p. 76). Each trigram is made up of three lines – the Yin being a broken line, the Yang an unbroken line – and symbolizes an aspect of the world. For instance, the first trigram, 'Heaven' (*tian*),

is made up of three unbroken lines; its related symbolism includes the 'creative force', the 'father', the 'head' of the body, and the direction it represents is the 'northwest'. The second trigram, 'Earth' (*kun*), is made of three broken lines, and its related symbolism includes the 'receptive force', the 'mother', the 'belly' and the direction it represents is the 'southwest'. When the trigrams combine with each other, they make up the sixty-four Hexagrams, which are the basis of the *Yi Jing* or *I Ching* ('Book of Changes'). A variety of Daoist divination methods evolved, employing plant stalks, coins and dice thrown to form trigram patterns as set out in divination manuals such as the *Yi Jing*.

An oracle bone fragment from the Shang dynasty.

changed or usurped by the advent of a new class of men who relied on scientific methods to cure ailments.

Shamanism does not often appear in the written sources that describe the ancient myths of China, though in Chapter Six we will encounter one example in Sima Qian's description of the propitiation of the God of the Yellow River by Ximen Bao (see p. 134). His account is typical of the Confucianist tendency among the scribal class to downplay or disregard shamanistic elements, making them not particularly reliable sources on Shamanism.

RELIGION IN MODERN CHINA

In the nineteenth and twentieth centuries, the introduction of western technologies made a huge difference to people living in the larger urban centres of China, and many of the popular beliefs and rituals associated with the old gods began to be looked down upon as 'superstitious practices'. In 1949, Mao Zedong led the Communist takeover of China, and in 1966 he launched the Cultural Revolution, which lasted for a decade. It was violent and destructive: many temples were denigrated as part of the 'old superstitions' and destroyed, and tales about traditional gods were forbidden – but not forgotten. After Mao's death in 1976, the proscription of the old faiths was relaxed, and temple fairs in rural communities were revived, where people brought their surplus goods for sale or barter. As the economy grew and private enterprises were no longer forbidden, people became wealthier and began donating to temples again. As a consequence, the temples have been rebuilt and the tales are being retold.

Tourists visiting the temple of Jing An in Shanghai. The temple was
first built in 247 CE and was moved to its current location in 1216.

Temples have also benefited from the rise of globalization in
the late twentieth and twenty-first centuries, becoming magnets for
tourists intrigued by Chinese traditions and culture. Local branches
of government have been quick to see the money-making possibili-
ties of reconstructed temples and their renewed festivities, taking
advantage of people's newfound desire to travel. Groups of tourists
from across the world are regaled with the local version of myths
and legends by government-funded tour guides. The visitors might
not look like the old pilgrims, but as long as they buy incense and
bow low, no one bothers to question their beliefs – they bring in
good money.

By contrast to the anti-religious sentiment in twentieth-century
mainland China, Hong Kong and Taiwan carried on much as they
had done before. In Taiwan many temples function as community

hubs as well as religious centres. Many western tourists are drawn to these ancient sanctuaries, and it is in such places that the gods and their altars – as described in the late imperial period by foreigners – can still be seen.

Since the ancient myths and stories have ceased to be a subject for opprobrium, many have found new life in television or cinema, often combining with science fiction or fantasy. These films, especially animated ones, are very popular. Myths are also referenced in the names of new scientific discoveries or technological endeavours. For instance, China's first Martian rover is named after the God of Fire, Zhurong, and the spacecrafts of China's lunar exploration programme are named 'Chang'e' after the lunar goddess herself. The first, Chang'e 1, was launched in 2007, and the most recent was Chang'e 5, China's first lunar sample-return mission, launched in 2020.

CHINA'S LITERARY TRADITIONS

The short-lived Qin dynasty (221–207 BCE) was the first to unite the states of China, but it wasn't until the subsequent Han dynasty (202 BCE–220 CE) came to power that the new imperial age truly began. Most of our earliest sources of the ancient myths were written during the Han period. When it comes to pre-Han sources, we are mainly left with the classics, such as the 'Five Classics' said to have been written by Confucius. The individual states were very local in content, so that *Chu Ci* ('Songs of Chu') represented only the songs of Chu. The earlier Zhou dynasty (*c.* 1046–256 BCE), which we might call the 'real' ancient China, has left little in the way of written sources, because not many people could read or write.

AN ORAL TRADITION

The myths of the classical era were part of an oral tradition, common knowledge that was seldom written down. Few people in ancient China knew how to read or write, and so passing on stories by telling them through the generations was the only way to keep them alive. It is also possible that people had no fear of the myths disappearing, since everyone already knew them. Yet stories preserved by word of mouth have a way of changing, and what is common knowledge at one time may be forgotten. More than two thousand years have

Wenchang: The God of Literature

The God of Literature was especially popular among the members of the scribal class – and particularly those about to take their examinations. According to Sima Qian's *Shiji* ('Records of the Grand Historian'), there were six stars above the Northern Dipper, where Wenchang had his abode. The god of these stars looked after the fate of every man. The Wenchang star as a god was an established figure from early Zhou times in the region of Shu, Sichuan Province. Later traditions associate him with the warrior Zhang Yazi, who lived under the Jin dynasty (266–420 CE) in Zitong, Sichuan Province. Zhang Yazi was said to have been killed in battle, and as a god dictated men's fortunes. In the Song dynasty, when the exams became more or less the only path for ambitious men to advance their standing, Zhang Yazi was elevated to become a God of Examinations.

The God of Literature, Wenchang,
with his servants.

passed, and much of what was not written down has been lost. Indeed, many written sources have also been lost. Some myths, however, seem to have survived practically unchanged, despite the passage of centuries.

Shortly before the Han dynasty, the reign of the literati began; that is, those who knew how to read and write. During the Warring States period of the Eastern Zhou dynasty (476–221 BCE), there was a rise in literacy among the members of the *shi* class. The *shi*, translated as 'knights' or 'gentlemen', formed the lesser aristocracy and were typically engaged in the military, but came to be educated in literary and philosophical matters and began to take on the role of 'secretaries' or 'chamberlains'. In this capacity they had greater opportunity to leverage power; they were not the masters, but rather the men whom the masters followed because they liked what was being said. Indeed, it became the order of the day to convince the ruler of what they said, rather than what their opponents said; a practical rather than a philosophical solution, and the Chinese have been very practical people all along.

The patchwork nature of the oral tradition and the written sources that have attempted to record it make it difficult to reconstruct the ancient myths. The Han-dynasty sources are not as true to the original myths as we would like. Firstly, because a great number of the people who could read and write – the *shi*, or scribal, class – were Confucianist in conviction, thus preferred history to myths. Secondly, no one person could have written down all the states' various versions of the ancient tales. Sima Qian wrote in the *Shiji*, 'Wherever I went, all of the village elders would point out for me sites of [Emperors] Huang Di, Yao and Shun. The traditions were certainly very different from each other…. I edited and selected those words which were the most appropriate'. Different accounts of the same stories often contradict each other, owing to the variant evolution of the lore in different places, among different people, and told in different dialects. Yet with few books surviving from pre-Han times, we are dependent on the Han sources.

What may seem surprising is that the nugget of these stories remains the same. Some of the earlier myths have survived in a form not so different from what we can gather from books written before the end of the Han dynasty. Even now, as most anthropologists and folklorists will testify, the younger generation still hear from their elders the same stories of the early myths, particularly at temple festivals, which people living in rural communities used to rely on for entertainment. This is partly because these stories were repeated at fixed points throughout the year and so they remained the same. In spite of the degradation of religion, actively censored as 'superstition' during the Cultural Revolution, many temples devoted to the gods of the early myths still survive in China. Those that have endured tend to have a special connection to their location, sometimes being where the god's cult first began. We have already seen the temple to the god Pangu on top of the mountain that bears his name in Henan Province; another example is the Renzu Temple, Shaanxi Province, where the ancient gods Nuwa and Fuxi (see p. 70) were worshipped, which is now crowded with both real pilgrims and tourists. Where myths have changed, the ancient traditions did not simply disappear overnight, but were overtaken gradually by other versions more relevant to the contemporary world: popular religious beliefs gained more prominence as time went on.

ANCIENT AND CLASSICAL SOURCES

Apart from glimpses of myths in works from the Zhou era, such as the *Shi Jing* ('Classic of Poetry'), we have a handful of written sources from the classical era. The most important of these are two books that are maddeningly incomplete: the *Shan Hai Jing* ('Classic of Mountains and Seas') and the *Tian Wen* ('Heavenly Questions'), both found in the *Chu Ci* ('Songs of Chu').

The *Shan Hai Jing* is a kind of mythical atlas; the only text from it that remains are captions accompanying various maps and illustrations of pre-Qin China. It provides laconic descriptions of the myths of ancient China, though it sometimes gives contradictory

Landscape from a Ming-dynasty edition of the *Shan Hai Jing* ('Classic of Mountains and Seas').

accounts. No one is sure when this work was produced, but it seems that it was created by more than one author and possibly composed from the Warring States period (476–221 BCE) to the Han dynasties (220 BCE–220 CE). The reclusive poet Tao Qian (365–427 CE), who lived during the Tang and Northern Song dynasties, said how much he enjoyed reading the *Shan Hai Jing*, but we do not know whether the edition he read included the original illustrations.

The *Tian Wen* ('Heavenly Questions') from the *Chu Ci* are attributed to the Chu poet and politician Qu Yuan (*c*. 340–278 BCE). In it the author poses a series of questions without any answers; again, perhaps these were popular knowledge, deemed unnecessary to write down. The *Heavenly Questions* are written in a very archaic language, and in fact probably pre-date even the poet Qu Yuan. It is

Writers in Isolation

Laozi, one of the greatest Daoist thinkers, was said to have lived in isolation in the countryside, and even Confucius found it difficult to settle down, travelling from state to state, failing to interest rulers in his philosophy. There is a strong tradition of isolation from society in Buddhism: monks often lived for decades alone in caves, meditating. Throughout China's history there are stories of such retreats from society and even in late traditional China, banishment to desolate northern wildernesses or unhealthy southern jungles was a common punishment. Even Confucianists who served in the government bureaucracy would praise escaping to the countryside in their poems, which often wistfully describe a lonely hut in the mountains with only birds and local fishermen for company. Similarly, the Daoist ideal of harmony with nature was best achieved in a rural setting.

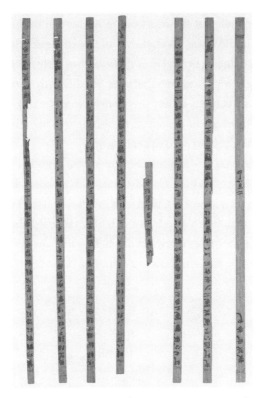

Annals written on bamboo strips from Yunmeng County, Qin dynasty.

possible that they were first written on bamboo strips. The ties that bind the writings together may have perished, so that the strips are not in the right order. Much of the esoteric wisdom contained in them is lost to us, and so there are many different interpretations of its questions. I have only included here those passages on which most scholars agree.

In addition to these two frustratingly fragmentary sources we have the *Huainanzi* ('Writings of the Huainan'), a collection of writings compiled at the court of Liu An, a ruler of the Huainan Kingdom. Liu An was an aristocrat of Daoist tendencies and the *Huainanzi* contains several of the best-known early myths. Liu An frames these myths as popular tales. He allegedly gathered one thousand scholars to collect these tales before writing his definitive version, which he presented to his nephew, the Emperor Wu (r. 141–87 BCE), in the second century BCE.

Sima Qian (*c.* 145–86 BCE), the famous Han historian who wrote the *Shiji* ('Records of the Grand Historian'), must not be ignored. He opened his account of China with the stories of the Five August Emperors and, like a good Confucianist, recorded these events as history rather than as myths, attributing to these emperors the founding of the Xia, Yin and Zhou dynasties. He was careful with his

Ming-dynasty illustration of the Han historian Sima Qian.

The Five August Emperors

Confucianist scholars such as Sima Qian historicized the five great gods associated with Daoism's Five Directions (see p. 24), recasting them as the Five August Emperors of ancient times. As with the gods, different textual sources list different gods and emperors as the five, but Huang Di (the Yellow Emperor) and Zhuanxu (his grandson) were always among them. In the *Huainanzi* (*c.* 139 BCE) the others are given as Yan Di (the God of Fire), Houtu (the earth deity), and Shaohao (the White Emperor). Sima Qian, however, lists the Five August Emperors as Huang Di, Zhuanxu, Di Ku (another grandson of Huang Di) and the Sage Kings Yao and Shun, all of whom we shall meet later.

A sixteenth-century silk painting of the Exalted Emperors
and the Gods of the Five Directions.

sources, sifting through them and accepting only what he believed to be historical. We know that he referred to the *Shang Shu* ('Book of Documents'), a work of political philosophy allegedly compiled by Confucius, but he also used sources of which we know nothing, since they are no longer extant.

Some of the ancient myths survived the Three Kingdoms period (220–280 CE), an era of fragmented states that followed the collapse of the Han, enduring into the reunification of the Chinese world under the Jin dynasty (266–420 CE). The most important of the Jin accounts of the myths is the *Soushen Ji* ('In Search of the Supernatural'), written by the historian Gan Bao (*c.* 350 CE) in Henan Province. These tales seem to be taken from the oral tradition. Sadly this book has been lost since about the fourteenth century, and is only known through its quotation in later works. The *Bo Wu Zhi* ('Records of Diverse Matters') by the poet and scholar Zhang Hua (232–300) and the *Shiyi Ji* ('Records of Forgotten Tales') by the Daoist scholar Wang Jia (d. 390) are likewise lost. These were all produced in the Jin dynasty, but they may have recorded oral traditions that had endured for many centuries.

Rather than only recounting the well-known legends that have come down to the present day, I have attempted to find the earliest occurring instances of the ancient myths in our sources, and where possible I have quoted them at length. This leads to quite a number of contradictions, since we don't have a Hesiod or Ovid to guide us, as we have for the Greek and Roman myths. But these many versions are the essence of the Chinese mythic world.

3

ORIGIN AND CREATION MYTHS

There are many Chinese myths concerning the origins of the world. The most popular written accounts involve the emergence of the cosmic forces of Yin and Yang from chaos, and the transformation of the body of Pangu, a semi-divine human, into the myriad things of this world.

YIN AND YANG

Yin and Yang are two fundamental forces in ancient Chinese philosophy, astrology and medicine. The Yin represents the feminine aspect, negative and receptive, all that is moist, dark, cool and shaded, while the Yang represents the masculine aspect, positive and active, being dry, bright, hot and sunny; the sun is referred to as the 'Great Yang'. Both these forces exist in all of us and in all things. Yin and Yang are buried deep in Chinese thinking and probably pre-date Daoism as we know it. They are present at the beginning of the *Tian Wen* ('Heavenly Questions') compiled in the third century BCE: 'How did they originate? And what do they do?' Answering these questions is a difficult task.

The Han-dynasty *Huainanzi* offers the following account of the creation of Yin and Yang:

Top: Yin Yang and the Eight Diagrams.
Above: A Qing-dynasty scroll painting of the Heavenly Horse
carrying the Yin Yang.

Long ago before heaven and earth existed, there were only images and no forms; all was obscure and dark, vague and unclear, shapeless and formless, with nothing able to enter or escape. There were two gods born of the darkness, ones that made heaven and earth, so vast that no one knew where they would end, so broad that no one knew where they would stop. They divided into Yin and Yang. They separated into the eight cardinal directions. The soft [Yin] and the hard [Yang] formed, and myriad things took shape. The turbid became the creatures of the world, and the lighter became humans.

In another section of the *Huainanzi*, *qi* – the vital energy of all things – is presented as a combination of Yin and Yang in their material form. It attributes the making of heaven and earth to *qi*: 'That which was pure and bright [Yang] formed heaven, and the turbid and heavy [Yi] formed earth. It was easy for the pure and bright to converge, but difficult for the turbid to congeal, therefore heaven was completed first and earth was fixed afterwards. The joint essences of heaven and earth produced Yin and Yang, the superior essences of Yin and Yang created the four seasons, the scattered essences of the four seasons created myriad things: the hot *qi* of accumulated Yang produced fire, the essence of fiery *qi* became the sun; the cold *qi* of accumulated Yin produced water, the essence of watery *qi* produced the moon. The overflowing essence of the sun and moon made the stars and planets. The sun, moon, and planets belong to heaven; while the rivers and rainwater, the dust and soil belong to earth.'

Above all gods and creator figures, not made of Yin or Yang, was Shangdi, the Supreme God, synonymous with heaven. The Supreme

God was invoked but not apparently active, without any anthropomorphic attributes, a sort of unique and eternal force, functioning as 'heaven' rather than occupying it.

PANGU

The earliest known written accounts of the story of creation come from the third century CE, when a Daoist named Xu Zheng described the metamorphosis of Pangu into the physical world, a process that took 36,000 years. Yet even Xu Zheng's works are lost to us and are

---

An Early Creation Account

The *Chu Boshu* ('Chu Silk Manuscript') was stolen from a tomb in Hunan, east of Changsha, in 1942, and is now in the Arthur M. Sackler Gallery in Washington, DC. The tomb was dated to about the middle of the Warring States period (476–221 BCE); thus this account precedes that written by Xu Zheng by some 500 years. The manuscript consists of three esoteric sections concerning ancient Chinese astronomy and astrology. Among the few legible passages is one concerning the beginning of the world: 'It was confusing and dark, without [...]; water, wind and rain were thus obstructed.' It offers a description of the chaos in which 'Long, long ago Baoxi [an alternate name for Fuxi; see p. 76] ... married Zuwei's granddaughter named Nu Tian. She gave birth to four [children], who then helped to put things in motion, making the transformations according to [Heaven's plan]'. It is not known who Zuwei and Nu Tian are, but Fuxi, here named Baoxi, appears in other texts as one of China's 'Three Divine Sovereigns', the mythical earliest rulers of the land, who we shall meet in Chapter Four.

Pangu separates heaven and earth to create the world. From a nineteenth-century edition of the Tang-dynasty *Tui Bei Quan Tu*, a collection of prophecies.

known only insofar as they are quoted in sources such as the *Yiwen Leiju* (624 CE), a Tang-dynasty encyclopaedia edited by Ouyang Xun. Before the story of Pangu was written down, it must have been passed down through the oral tradition, morphing over time and in different places so that many versions of the story now exist, but the fundamentals remain the same: the world began in chaos, the sky and earth as muddled as the contents of an egg, and Pangu came into being between them. After eighteen thousand years, heaven and earth separated. The clear Yang became the heaven, and the thick Yin became the earth. Pangu lay between them and he changed nine times a day; his wisdom became greater than heaven, his ability went beyond that of earth. Each day, the sky grew higher by ten feet, the earth grew thicker by ten feet, and Pangu grew taller by ten feet. And so it continued for another eighteen thousand years, until the sky reached its full height and the earth reached its lowest depth.

When Pangu died, his body was transformed into the universe. His breath became the wind and clouds, his voice the thunder. His left eye became the sun, his right eye the moon. His head, arms and legs became the four cardinal points and the five mountains. His blood became the rivers, his sinews the features of the land, his flesh the earth's soil. His hair and beard became the stars, the hairs on his skin grass and trees, his teeth and bones became metal and stones, his marrow pearls and jade. His sweat became rain; even the parasites on his body touched by the wind became the multitude of people.

Although Pangu was simply born into chaos, he has become rooted in Chinese cultural consciousness as a creator-god himself. There are many versions of the story: one version says that he took an axe and cut the egg-like chaos into two halves; another relates that he kept the earth and sky apart by taking the form of a huge

Worship of Pangu

Several temples were built for Pangu, especially along the coastal provinces, where he was worshipped as a benevolent deity. In Henan Province, a mountain was named after him, perhaps before Tang or Song times. At its summit sits a large temple, where pilgrims gather even today at the beginning of March, when his festivities are celebrated with the performance of plays and incense offerings. Since Pangu is said to be in charge of rain, the area around his temple reputedly does not suffer from drought.

A Qing-dynasty ink drawing of Pangu after completing the creation of the world.

pillar between them. As well as Pangu, this account of creation introduces us to another key concept in Chinese cosmology: the ideal balance of Yin and Yang.

THE HEAVENLY BODIES

The orthodox version of the tale of the creation of the earth, sun and moon is as follows:

> Beyond the south-east sea there lay the kingdom of Xihe.
> Xihe was the wife of the god Di Jun and she gave birth
> to the ten suns. There was a great world-tree called the
> Fusang, a mulberry tree in the sea in the east. Each sun

contained a three-legged crow. Nine of the sun crows
roosted in the lower branches of the Fusang, one sun in
the high branch. Each bird bore its own sun in turn to the
top of the tree to take its place in the journey across the
sky driven by Xihe, who acted as their charioteer. The suns
came out in turn, one after the other. When each had
crossed the sky, they were carried back to the mulberry
tree where Xihe bathed them in the boiling Gan ('sweet')
River, and the sun dried them out in the branches of the
mulberry tree.

In this tale there are ten suns, which was the number of days of
the week according to the old Chinese reckoning. They imagined
the suns as resting in a world-tree, which the ancient Chinese per-
ceived as a mulberry, and their mother (or charioteer) took them
out one after the other. As the *Shan Hai Jing* ('Classic of Mountains
and Seas') puts it, 'Beyond the southern sea, near the Gan River is
the Kingdom of Xihe. There is a woman named Xihe, she is now
bathing the suns in the Gulf of Gan. Xihe is the wife of Di Jun, she
bore ten suns.' It fell to Yi the Archer to save the world from the
scorching effects of ten suns, by shooting down nine of them.

YI THE ARCHER

Yi (or Hou Yi) was one of the most popular gods and it is not hard to
see why. In an agricultural community, the threat of drought was real
and its consequences harshly felt. Both the *Huainanzi* and the *Shan
Hai Jing* record that it was Yi the Archer who rid the world of the

Yi the Archer prepares to shoot down nine of the ten suns.
From a Qing-dynasty edition of the *Tian Wen* ('Heavenly Questions').

surplus of scorching suns, thus staving off the potential for disaster that they brought. Di Jun, a powerful god, was at first reluctant to allow this, because the suns were his children, but he relented and gave Yi 'a red-coloured bow and arrows with white streamers. He told him with this bow Yi could assist the people in the kingdom below. Yi began to aid the world below and rid them of myriad difficulties that they suffered'. As the *Tian Wen* ('Heavenly Questions') tells us, 'God on high sent Yi, to erase the calamities of the people of Xia'. It is a story of the good that gods can do for mankind.

Another version involves the great leader Yao: 'One day the ten suns came out at once. They scorched the sheaves of grain, killing plants and trees, so that people had no food.' Monsters appeared,

More than one Yi

The orthodox account of Yi tells us of the man (whom we meet as a god) who shot down the surplus suns, was married to Chang'e, and who died at the hand of his rival Feng Meng. This is the Yi that most ancient Chinese people would recognize as the saviour of humanity. There were, however, other versions of Yi, like Yi of the 'eastern barbarians', a proto-Yue people. An account from the *Zuo Zhuan* ('Zuo Tradition'), a commentary on the *Chunqiu* ('Spring and Autumn Annals'), describes him as a king of the Xia dynasty, 'who took advantage of his archery skills, neglecting public affairs and indulging in hunting game in the field'. His subjects were not impressed: 'One day his clansman all assassinated him, and they cooked his corpse in order to give to his sons to eat' – a grisly death, which would not appear in any orthodox telling. It is possible that Yi was a name for anyone who was good at archery.

A scroll painting of the imperial bodyguard Shanyinbao, a skilled Qing archer.

Chasing the Sun

The *Shan Hai Jing* ('Classic of Mountains and Seas') tells us how Kuafu, a grandson of the earth deity Houtu, decided one day to challenge the sun. Kuafu lived in the wilderness, on a mountain called Chengdu Zaitian. He had two yellow snakes in his ears and two in his hands. One day, wanting to prove his supreme strength, he decided 'to chase the sun and catch it where it set'. But he quickly became exhausted and 'felt so thirsty that he drank up the water from the Yellow River and the Wei River, which was not enough for him; he wanted to drink all the water from the Great Lake, but before he reached it, he died of thirst. His walking stick transformed into a forest of peach trees'.

'Kuafu chased the sun' is an ancient idiom in the Chinese vernacular, sometimes used to criticize people for overestimating their own ability – *kuafu* means 'braggart' or 'boastful man' – but also to praise them for their persistence and toughness. Kuafu is worshipped to this day in Lingbao County, Henan Province, as part of the local pantheon.

bringing death and plagues with them. The people's leader, Yao (see p. 107), ordered Yi the Archer to shoot down the monsters and the ten suns. The crows in each sun died and their feathers fell out. There was then much rejoicing amongst the people, who were once more able to get on with their lives, and they made Yao their emperor.

Yet Yi had angered Di Jun by killing his sons rather than remonstrating with them, so Yi and his wife, Chang'e, were banished forever from the heavens, the abode of the gods in Mount Kunlun. Yi went to find help from Xiwang Mu, the Queen Mother of the West (see p. 138). She gave him an elixir that granted immortality. Upon his return, Yi told his wife that he had the elixir, but would wait for an opportunity to take it. He left Chang'e with the elixir, trusting her with everything. But she had other ideas and stole the elixir, thus taking from Yi his chance at regaining immortality.

Yi remained on earth, no longer a god. He took as his pupil Feng Meng, who came to rival his skill with a bow; but realizing that he could never beat his master, Feng Meng clubbed Yi to death with a weapon made out of peach wood. So died the Archer Yi; but for his services to mankind, he was deified, becoming Zongbu.

Peach Wood

Feng Meng's use of peach wood for his deadly club may be symbolically connected with exorcism. The Chinese for 'peach', *tao*, is a homophone for the word 'to expel'; thus perhaps the peach wood was used to 'expel' noxious influences. The peach wood club was known as a *zhongkui*, the term later used for the name of the demon-slayer Zhong Kui who was not, therefore, a mythicized historical figure but the transformation of a weapon. Peaches were symbols of longevity, often depicted on ceramics and textiles.

A Qing-dynasty dish decorated with peaches and pomegranates.

THE MOON

There were twelve moons in the lunar myth, derived from the twelve divisions of the Chinese calendar year. In the *Shan Hai Jing* ('Classic of Mountains and Seas') we are introduced to another of Emperor Di Jun's wives, Changxi, mother of these moons: 'There is a woman, she is now bathing the moons. It is Emperor Di Jun's wife, her name is Changxi. She bore twelve moons and has begun to bathe them.' In yet another version, we are told that: 'In the middle of the great wilderness, there is a mountain called Feng Zu Yumen (literally, 'the Jade Gate'; it is also called *Riyue shan*, 'the Mountain of the Sun and Moon', later in the same chapter) where the sun and moon go in and out.'

Changxi's name in Chinese phonology is very close to that of the better-known moon goddess, Chang'e, the misbehaving wife of Yi the Archer. Some scholars think they originated from the same lunar goddess. Whether or not that is the case, it highlights the variability in our sources, where there may be differing numbers of moons.

Chang'e was originally called Heng'e, but her name was changed to avoid infringing the taboo of using the name of Liu Heng, the Emperor Wen (r. 180–157 BCE). The two words, *heng* and *chang*, both mean 'everlasting'.

Chang'e and the Moon

Yi and Chang'e were banished from the heavens because Yi had shot down the suns, and on earth they ceased to be immortals. Yi climbed, with great difficulty, up Mount Kunlun, the dwelling-place of all the gods, to ask Xiwang Mu for her elixir of immortality. She granted it to him, and when he returned home he entrusted it to his wife.

The moon goddess Chang'e holding Master Rabbit
and conversing with the goddess Ch'ing-nu, Qing dynasty.

But Chang'e remembered when she dwelt with the gods in heaven,
and decided to steal the elixir. She swallowed it all, and felt herself
floating into the air. Deciding not to return to Mount Kunlun, where
everyone would know she was a thief, she floated up to the moon,
which she knew was uninhabited except for a cassia tree, a frog and
a rabbit. Chang'e was forever after identified with the moon. Her
ongoing significance in China today can be seen in the name of the
Chang'e spacecrafts, which have been sent on various missions to
the moon between 2007 and 2020.

The Moon Festival

After the fourth century CE Chang'e receives a more sympathetic treatment, and is often cited as a beautiful woman who lives on the moon. In later tradition, the name Chang'e is often used for the moon itself. Today at the Moon Festival (also called the Mid-Autumn Festival), on the fifteenth day of the eighth month of the lunar calendar, when the moon is at its roundest, most Chinese families celebrate by making or buying 'mooncakes' stuffed with bean paste and sometimes an egg in the middle. Many families also buy effigies of Master Rabbit, another mythical inhabitant of the moon.

A seventeenth-century embroidery of Master Rabbit,
who accompanied Chang'e to the moon.

THE STARS

The stars are mentioned little in the classical Chinese myths. This is strange considering how keenly the Chinese observed the sky at night. Two fourth-century BCE astronomers, Gan De and Shi Shen, left books listing hundreds of stars and constellations. These books were in the imperial libraries of the Han dynasty, and were mentioned by Sima Qian in his *Shiji*, but have been since lost.

The only mention of stars in books produced before the Han dynasty were references to a myth about two brothers with a fierce rivalry. The *Zuo Zhuan* ('Zuo Tradition'), a commentary on the *Chunqiu* ('Spring and Autumn Annals'), tells us: 'Long ago Gao Xin [another name for the god Di Ku] had two sons. The elder was called Yan Bo, the younger Shi Chen. They lived in a vast forest. They could not abide each other and they would fight with shield and dagger-axe, and made attacks on each other. [Di Ku] was displeased, and moved Yan Bo to Shang Qiu, putting him in charge of the Chen star…. And he moved Shi Chen so he took charge of the Shen star.' The Shen and Chen stars lay on opposite sides of Orion, where the brothers remained safely out of each other's reach.

The Cowherd and the Weaving Girl

For Han poets this myth served as a metaphor for estranged lovers, far apart and suffering. The only other significant reference to stars in Chinese mythology is the story of the Weaving Girl, which first appears in the *Shi Jing* ('Classic of Poetry') and seems to derive from the tenth or ninth century BCE. The Weaving Girl is mentioned as the star who was far apart from her lover, the Draught Ox, who transformed as time went by into the Cowherd.

The Weaving Girl floats away into the sky
as the Cowherd calls to her.

The story of 'The Cowherd and the Weaving Girl', as it is popularly known now, can be traced no earlier than the eleventh century CE. It is more detailed and shows the influence of later legends.

There was a Cowherd who lived alone after his elder brothers gave him his inheritance from his father, which was in the form of a single ox. However, the ox was no ordinary creature, but a god who had been banished from Heaven for telling the people to eat three meals a day rather than one meal every three days, which was what the Supreme God had ordered, but he had been foolish enough to trust the message to the stupidity of an ox. 'You had better go down to earth and help the people by ploughing for them.' And so the Ox God had ended up as the lone inheritance of the Cowherd. He now said to the Boy, 'You have been good to me, and I see that you are a hard worker. Go to the pool yonder and hide there. You will see the Heavenly Maidens descend to wash themselves; take the clothes of one whom you like, and she will be obliged to stay with you.'

The Cowherd did as he was told, and the Heavenly Maiden turned out to be a Weaving Girl. She had to stay with the Cowherd, but she turned into a very good wife who gave two children to the Cowherd, and wove the most beautiful things, which the Cowherd was able to sell. One day she came upon the clothes that had been stolen from her long ago, she put them on, and floated away into the sky. When the Cowherd realized what had happened, he put his two children into baskets on either side of a carrying pole, and chased after her, calling to her with the children. But the Supreme God was reluctant to see the Cowherd getting nearer to her, so with his hand he drew a Heavenly River, the Milky Way, between the two of them and the Cowherd was forever separated from the Weaving Girl. Yet the Supreme God took pity on them, and once a year on the night of the seventh day of the seventh month, all the magpies in the sky go to form a bridge over the Milky Way for them to meet.

Modern Influences on Ancient Tales

This version of the story given here is the most popular. It first
appeared in school textbooks that were edited in the 1950s, but in
recent years, doubt has been cast on the episode that describes the
Cowherd choosing the woman while she bathes with others in the
pool. This would have been very improper behaviour, and indeed
older versions of the legend only tell of the Cowherd stealing one or
two garments – not gazing at naked women. It is thought that this
particular incident came from the modern Peking opera *Tian He Pei*
('Love on either side of the Milky Way'), first performed around 1924,
inserted to please the modern audience. Retellings of the newer
version, based on the opera, attracted greater audiences and so it
became the accepted version, and the editors of the schoolbooks
used the later version without thinking.

You may see a bright star, called the Vega, in the constellation of
Lyra on one side of the Milky Way, and on the other you see another
bright star, Altair, with two smaller stars beside it in the constellation
Aquila. These are the Cowherd and the Weaving Girl, who meet only
once a year, on the night of the seventh day of the seventh month.

Many other sayings have grown up around this date. Even today
the seventh day of the seventh month is celebrated as the *Qiqiao*
('Seven Cleverness'), and girls follow the tradition of showing off
their embroidery skills, much as the Weaving Girl might have done.
It is also the day where girls might find an image of their future
husband, dimly seen in a mirror.

NUWA: CREATOR OF HUMANITY

Humanity did not come into being when the earth and the heavenly bodies were first created by Pangu and the cosmic forces of Yin and Yang. One story tells how Nuwa, celebrated today as a mother goddess, moulded men and women from the yellow earth. She began by crafting them individually. This was a laborious process, and so she dragged a cord through the mud and then shook it: pieces of mud dropped down, and these too became people. As a source dating to the second century CE has it, 'People say that when heaven and earth opened and unfolded, humankind did not exist. Nuwa kneaded yellow earth and fashioned human beings. Though she worked feverishly, she did not have enough strength to finish her task, so she drew a cord in a furrow through the mud and lifted it out to make human beings. That is why rich aristocrats are the human beings made from yellow earth, while ordinary poor commoners are the human beings made from the cord's furrow.'

Mending Heaven

As well as crafting humanity from the yellow clay of the Chinese plains, Nuwa is celebrated for mending heaven when it broke. It was believed that the sky, which was round and covered the square earth, was held up by four pillars. In some traditions these pillars were believed to be the limbs of Pangu; in others, they were mountains at the four poles. The story goes that the water god Gonggong butted into the mythical Mount Buzhou, the pillar of the northwest, during a fight with Zhuanxu, grandson of the Yellow Emperor (see p. 102). The pillar collapsed, with disastrous consequence for all the world. As the *Huainanzi* tells us:

The mother goddess Nuwa repairs the pillar of heaven.
From a Ming-dynasty edition of the *Shan Hai Jing*.

The four pillars that held up the sky at the poles collapsed, all nine of the provinces were split and broken. The sky did not completely cover the earth, and the earth did not lie under the circumference of heaven. Fires blazed out of control and could not be extinguished, and water overflowed, covering huge expanses and would not recede. Fierce animals devoured the people, and great raptors seized the young and old who were vulnerable.

At this Nuwa smelted five-coloured stones to mend the blue firmament. She severed the feet of a large turtle to support the four poles, and killed a black dragon to save the people of China. She gathered the ashes of reeds to stop the flood. The blue firmament was mended, the four poles were straightened, the flooding water receded, so that the people of China could be at peace again. The ferocious beasts died and the population revived. They bore the square earth upon their backs, and hugged the round sky above them.

Examining these achievements, we find that they reach up to the ninefold heavens and down to the deep earth; [her] fame resounds through the later generations, its brilliance spreads over all things. Nuwa rode in a chariot of thunder, yoked to four dragons, to float among the clouds with gods and spirits, she climbed to the ninefold heavens and entered the gates. Nuwa sought audience with [the Supreme] God. She reported her work, then rested there with dignity. She did not boast of her achievements, concealing her own god-like genius following the dictates of heaven and earth.

In this story, we see the cultural impact of the constant risk of flood in China. A version of the Nuwa myth in the third chapter of the *Huainanzi* gives the reason that all the rivers in China flow to the east: 'Heaven tilted to the northwest, and thus the sun, moon, and all the stars shifted in that direction, earth became empty in the southeast. Thus the waters and the mountainous soil subsided in that direction.' The Yellow River flooded frequently and often disastrously right up until very recently. For this reason it has been called 'China's Sorrow', as well as the 'Mother River' – both cradle and destroyer of civilization. The Yangtze, hundreds of miles lower than its northern counterpart and the longest river in Asia, caused catastrophic floods every fifty years or so before the construction of modern dams. Not surprisingly, the threat of floods was an ever-present anxiety in people's minds, which found expression in myths, as we shall explore further in Chapter Six. Unlike the account of the Great Flood given in the Bible, there is no suggestion in the Chinese flood myths that the deluge was a punishment for the people's sins. In the Chinese version, the flood just happens, in the way that the Yellow River swells with the spring melt of the snows in the upper reaches of the Himalayas.

Patroness of Marriage

Perhaps because of her role as 'the mother of humanity', Nuwa became associated closely with marriage. The *Du Yi Zhi* ('A Treatise on Extraordinary and Strange Things'), a Tang-dynasty work by Li Rong (*c.* ninth century CE) likely based on older traditions, tells us how Nuwa and her brother became the model for marriage: 'In ancient times, when the world first began, there was Nuwa and her brother, and they lived on Mount Kunlun [see p. 137]. At that time there was no humankind. They decided to become husband and wife, but they felt ashamed. The brother climbed up Mount Kunlun with his sister and prayed. "If heaven wants us to become husband and wife, then let the smoke from our burning bands come together, if not, then let the smoke scatter." At this the smoke gathered together. The young woman went to be with her brother. Yet she plaited straw into a fan to hide her face. Even now, when a man takes a wife, she holds a fan in memory of what happened then.' This account does not name the brother; some say that it was Fuxi (see p. 76).

A slightly different version of this myth is told among many peoples of south China, especially the Miao. The siblings Fuxi and

A Han-dynasty brick-rubbing depicting a mythical scene with Fuxi and Nuwa, who appear on the bottom register, with entwined, snakelike tails.

Modern Worship of Nuwa

There are many temples to Nuwa across China, some quite modest in size. In Huaiyang County, Henan Province, Nuwa is still honoured at the temple of Renzu, where she and Fuxi are celebrated as the ancestors of all people. Nuwa's role is remembered with a special dance during the temple fair, which takes place every year in honour of the pair. Pilgrims sing folksongs that tell the story of Nuwa and Fuxi's founding of the human race.

A silk painting of Nuwa and Fuxi entwined, third to eighth century CE.

Nuwa had been told to watch Lei Gong, the God of Thunder, who had been imprisoned by their father. On no account were they to give the prisoner anything to drink. Nuwa, however, took pity when the God of Thunder showed signs of extreme thirst and gave him some water, which he then used to melt the bars of his cage and escape. Before he vanished, he gave the girl the seeds of a gourd, telling her that she and her brother should get into the gourd when it had grown. Afterwards, there was rain non-stop for days and weeks, and the brother and sister got into the gourd, which floated on the flood. When the flood ceased, the brother and sister married, and gave birth to those who became humankind.

MOTHER GODDESSES

We encounter very few goddesses in the paternalistic accounts of the myths of China; the exceptions are mother goddesses, such as Nuwa. According to Confucianism, within the family unit the mother was often as important as the father. We therefore find that the mothers of gods or the founders of dynasties were named. Often heroes were conceived under supernatural circumstances, thematically similar to virgin births in western mythologies and religions. Such stories hint that matriarchy may have been the dominant system in ancient China. The following myths are but a few of those that refer to virgin births.

Jian Di: Mother of the Shang Dynasty

The Shang dynasty (also known as the Yin dynasty, *c.* 1600–1046 BCE), the first great Bronze Age civilization of China, had a legendary female ancestor, Jian Di. She was the second wife of Di Ku, who is often named as one of the Five August Emperors. Her son, Xie (also called Qi), founder of the Shang dynasty, was born by a miraculous conception. This myth is told in various ancient texts and poems, dating as far back as the sixth century BCE. The Han historian Sima Qian records one version of the story in the *Annals of the Yin*: 'As for Xie [the founder] of the [Shang] dynasty, his mother was called Jian Di. She was a daughter of the Yu Song clan, and the secondary wife of [Di] Ku. One day she and two other women went to bathe, and she saw a black bird lay an egg. Jian Di took it and swallowed it. For this reason she became pregnant and gave birth to Xie.' The *Tian Wen* ('Heavenly Questions') in the *Chu Ci* also mention Jian Di and talk of the 'swallow' that brought her the egg.

The mid-Han *Shiyi Ji* ('Records of Forgotten Tales') records a variant of the myth in which the egg dropped by the black bird had the words 'eight hundred' inscribed upon it. That night Jian Di had a dream in which a mother goddess told her, 'You possess this egg, and you will give birth to a great son'. The story goes that Xie was born and the dynasty that he founded lasted for 800 years, just as had been predicted (not as implausible a prediction as in some myths, given that the dynasty did in reality endure for some 550 years).

Jiang Yuan: Mother of the Zhou Dynasty

Like the Shang dynasty, its successor, the Zhou (1046–256 BCE), also had a mythical ancestress, Jiang Yuan. She was the first consort of the god Di Ku, and gave birth to the god Houji, founder of the Zhou dynasty. Here, again, the pregnancy was brought about through a miraculous conception, as we are told in a lengthy poetic account *Shengmin* ('Giving Birth to the People') from the sixth-century BCE *Shi Jing* ('Classic of Poetry'). After offering a sacrifice to the Supreme God to overcome her childlessness, Jiang Yuan trod on a giant footprint left by the god. In due course she gave birth to a son, but she regarded the child as 'unlucky' and tried to abandon it to its death, first in a narrow lane:

> But the sheep and oxen protected him and fed him.
> Jiang Yuan then tried to place him in a forest,
> But he was protected by woodcutters there.
> She then placed him on the cold ice,
> But birds covered him with their wings,
> When the birds went away
> Houji began to wail.

At this point Jiang Yuan relented and brought up the child, who would go on to give China its staple crop, millet, and – according to Sima Qian – found the Zhou dynasty. Rituals and legends about Jiang Yuan were recorded in the 1920s in Shaanxi Province, where there is a temple to the goddess in Wenxi County. Here in March of each year, a temple fair would take place and operas about her would be performed.

Houji: The Millet God

The fertile, alluvial plains of northern China, fed by the Yellow River, were ideal for the growing of millet, one of the two staple crops – along with rice in the south – that underpinned the growth of Chinese civilization. It is no surprise, therefore, to find that the 'millet god', Houji, rose to prominence in the Chinese pantheon. Sima Qian (c. 145–86 BCE) gave an account of Houji in the 'Basic Annals of Zhou' (in his *Shiji*), believing him to be the founding ancestor of the house of Zhou, which succeeded the Shang dynasty and dominated China from about 1045 BCE.

In spite of his early neglect, he grew healthy and large, and when he began to feed himself he took to planting many things – beans and millet, melons and gourds – and they all flourished. When he grew up, he planted all kinds of crops and different types of millet, and inaugurated sacrifices to the Supreme God. He died and was buried in the wilderness of Duguang, where the crops grow abundantly, and the weather is mild all year round. Houji's role in the pantheon of Chinese gods is very similar to that of Shennong, the God of Agriculture (see p. 80). It may represent a different version of the same myth.

4

THE FIRST GODS

The gods of ancient China are hard to trace before the Han dynasty; sometimes we know only their names, and it is likely that many have been lost entirely to obscurity. We find, for example, many named deities in the *Shan Hai Jing* ('Classic of Mountains and Seas'), but few have narratives attached to them. Unlike the immortal deities of many western traditions and pantheons, the Chinese gods seem to have had a limited life expectancy: they would die, though often at a greater age than humans. In this tradition, perhaps we see the influence of Confucianism. The Han-dynasty historian Sima Qian (*c.* 145–86 BCE) was the first to make a systematic study of Huang Di (the Yellow Emperor; see p. 82), turning him into a historical figure, and a fit founder of the Chinese people. According to the Confucianists who wanted to historicize Huang Di, he lived around the twenty-sixth or twenty-fifth centuries BCE, and died aged 113. It is hard to know whether this applied to all the gods, both in their early worship and their later canonizations; our sources do not make it clear. Here I have collected the best-known early gods, whose stories survive well enough to allow their reconstruction.

THE THREE DIVINE SOVEREIGNS

In Chinese thought the number three is an expression of perfection and totality. During the Han dynasty, when a rationalized chronology of Chinese ancient history was codified, the triad of heaven, earth, and humanity were seen as the three great spiritual forces of the universe. This was a rather abstract conception, however, for Confucianist thinkers. Three prestigious figures from the mythological tradition were therefore chosen as the Three Divine Sovereigns (*Sanhuang*), the earliest rulers of China, godlike figures who passed their essential skills and knowledge onto humankind. Because of these gifts to civilization, they are often referred to as 'culture heroes'. Although the list varies, Fuxi, as the first named god who was supposed to have created humanity out of primeval chaos, was always included. So too was Shennong, the god of farming and medicine. The third could be Nuwa, the mother goddess, who we met in the previous chapter; Zhurong, a fire god (see p. 103); Suirenshi (p. 81), who introduced to humanity the making of fire and cooked food; or Huang Di, the Yellow Emperor.

FUXI

Fuxi consistently appears in pre-Han sources as one of the *Sanhuang*. He must, therefore, have been of great importance, but very little is left of his stories in the surviving texts. His name appears in a variety of forms, written with different characters that had the same or nearly the same pronunciation. For example, he is called 'Baoxi' in the *Chu Boshu* ('Chu Silk Manuscript') (see box, p. 50), and in

A nineteenth-century ink drawing of Fuxi-Taihao holding the Yin Yang symbol.

Taihao

In pre-Han times, Taihao was often included as one of the gods of the Five Directions (see p. 25), governing in particular the east and spring, and associated with the element wood. He was assisted by the god Goumang in these aspects (Goumang was in some sources simply a title for an official in charge of timber). During the Han dynasty, Taihao was gradually identified with the god Fuxi, and they merged as Fuxi-Taihao.

Fuxi-Taihao is today worshipped at 'the tomb of Taihao' at Renzu Temple in Huaiyang County, Henan Province. Huaiyang is believed to be the capital of Fuxi-Taihao's mythical kingdom. Every February, a festival takes place to celebrate the god's birthday.

the Han dynasty he was given the name and attributes of another pre-Han god called Taihao, becoming Fuxi-Taihao.

Fuxi was one of the great culture heroes: he was credited with inventing, among other things, the arts of hunting, music and divination through *bagua* ('the Eight Trigrams', see box, p. 32). He invented fishing by observing how a spider casts its web, teaching men to make nets like spiders' webs and place them in the water to catch fish. He may have been a hunting god when the Chinese were hunter-gatherers – wild animals were a prime source of food before settled agriculture became dominant in China. Fuxi also invented musical instruments, such as the *guqin* or zither, which in its modern form is a seven-stringed, plucked instrument.

Fuxi overlooking the Eight Trigrams of divination. From a nineteenth-century Korean album of 144 historical and legendary Chinese figures.

Fuxi is mostly remembered for his association with Nuwa (see p. 66) in myths derived from the ancient oral tradition. They alone were saved after the Flood, and as husband and wife peopled the world. They are often represented as human from the waist up, with the tails of dragons or snakes, in Han-dynasty or earlier stone carvings and in pictures drawn on silk. This has led some scholars to speculate that Fuxi was the son of Lei Gong, the Thunder God, who likewise always appears with a human upper body and dragon lower body. Nuwa is often shown with a compass and Fuxi with a builder's square, indicating belief in their construction of the earth, since in myth the earth is square and heaven is round.

The numerous artistic depictions of Fuxi and Nuwa made the scholar and poet Wen Yiduo (1899–1946) think that at the height of the Han dynasty they were the most important gods. This changed in the third century CE, when Pangu was seen as the founder of the world.

Fuxi was born at the Renzu ('Ancestor of All Humans') Temple complex in Shaanxi Province, once known as the Tomb of Taihao but now regarded as a temple to Fuxi and Nuwa. The temple has been reconstructed many times, and one legend related by locals in Huaiyang concerns the founder of the Ming dynasty (1368–1644), Zhu Yuanzhang. Before Zhu became emperor of the Ming dynasty, he was being chased by his enemies and he hid in the temple's ruins. In his desperation, he promised Fuxi that he would rebuild the temple in exchange for the god's protection. Spiders came and spun their webs all over the door, and thus Zhu eluded capture, as those who were chasing him thought that no one could have entered the building for a long time. Once emperor, he fulfilled his promise to rebuild the temple.

SHENNONG

'Shennong thrashed all the plants with a red whip, and knew thoroughly their blandness, their toxicity, their effect of coldness or heat; their smell being the guide. He sowed the myriad grains. For this reason everyone called him the farmer god.' So goes the account of the ox-headed Shennong in the *Soushen Ji* ('In Search of the Supernatural'), compiled around 350 CE. The *Huainanzi* elaborates: 'In ancient times, the people fed on plants and drank water from rivers, they picked fruit from trees and ate the meat from shellfish. At that time they frequently suffered and were injured by poisons. So Shennong taught the people to sow the five grains.' Agriculture was of fundamental importance in ancient China, and so Shennong, like Fuxi, was always one of the Three Divine Sovereigns.

The *Huainanzi* also tells us that Shennong ingested the seventy types of herbs known to humankind, and thus was able to teach people how to differentiate between them: 'He tried the flavour of all the plants, and the sweetness or brackishness of all the rivers and springs, letting the people know what to avoid or accept. At that time he suffered poisoning seventy times a day.' In this way Shennong discovered medicine, and China's first medicinal manual, the *Shennong Bencai Jing* ('Classic Pharmacopeia of Shennong'), is attributed to him, though in reality this work was probably written in the third century BCE.

But even the god was not infallible. He finally died after ingesting the poison from a small yellow flower before he could detoxify. This plant is now known as the *duan chang cao*, 'the intestine-breaking grass'. He was worshipped in later China. Shennong is often confused with Yan Di, God of Fire, possibly because Shennong was sometimes

A sixteenth-century illustration of the divine farmer Shennong chewing
a branch, indicating his role as discoverer of medicinal plants.

called the 'God of the Burning Wind', referring to the scorching of
the land in the days when 'slash and burn' agriculture was practised.

SUIRENSHI

The fire-maker Suirenshi's prominence, like Shennong's, can be
linked to the cultural importance of food production. He discovered
that fire could be created by drilling on wood. The *Tai Ping Yu Lan*
('Readings of the Taiping Era'), one of the great works commissioned
by the Song dynasty in the tenth century CE, records that he was the
first person to observe a bird pecking at the fire-bearing wood of a
legendary tree called the Sui-tree: '[A sage] happened to rest below
the tree. There was a bird rather like an owl. And when it pecked the
tree with its beak, then suddenly fire shot out. The sage was moved by
this, so he took a small twig to drill for fire, and he was a man of Sui.'

A print of the fire-maker Suirenshi, who introduced fire and taught humanity how it could be used for warmth and cooking.

He taught the people what he learned, and they began to use fire for warmth and for cooking, an essential step on the path to civilization. He is the most benign of the gods of fire; Yan Di (see p. 96) is all show, and Zhurong (p. 103), the fire that destroys, is the most pernicious.

HUANG DI

Huang Di, or the Yellow Emperor, is one of the best-known gods in Chinese mythology, and also the most important figure of the Three Divine Sovereigns and the Five August Emperors (see box, p. 45). Literally, he should be called the 'Yellow God' (*huang* means 'yellow' or 'glorious' in Chinese, and *di* means 'god'), but he has been translated so often into English as the Yellow Emperor that I shall refer to him by this well-known name. He was the most warlike of the gods, defeating all his rivals, though in later traditions he was seen as a peaceable and moral ruler.

Huang Di's mother, Fubao, who is worshipped as a goddess in her own right, conceived him after seeing a bright flash of light in the constellation Ursa Major. The *Shizi*, written during the Warring States period but known to us only through sections included in later *leishu* (encyclopaedias), tells us that 'Fubao saw a great bolt of lightning encircle one of the stars in the [constellation] of the Great Bear; it was so bright that it lit up the area nearby. Then Fubao became pregnant, and after twenty-five months gave birth to Huang Di' on the mound that bears his other name, Xuanyuan. Fubao was

A Ming-dynasty woodcut of the Yellow Emperor Huang Di.

the consort of Shaodian; and so Huang Di was regarded as his son. Huang Di's main consort is Leizu, whom we meet as the deity who first encouraged sericulture (silk production). Many legendary figures traced their lineage to Huang Di, among them Zhuanxu, another of the Five August Emperors, and Gun and Yu, the heroes

Qin Shi Huangdi: First Emperor of China

Ruthless and a brilliant organizer, King Zheng of Qin, one of the competing states of China during the Warring States period, conquered his rivals and created a unified state in 221 BCE, declaring himself Qin Shi Huangdi: 'The First August Emperor'. Previously the title *wang* had been used to denote a ruler or king of a state. After his triumph in military conquests, Zheng deliberately arrogated to himself the attributes of the mythical deity Huang Di, 'the Great and Impressive God'. After his reign, *huangdi* became the title for all rulers of imperial China.

Qin Shi Huangdi, the First Emperor of China. Nineteenth-century ink drawing.

who controlled the flood (see p. 113). In a much later tradition, he is seen as the common ancestor of the Han or Chinese people, who refer to themselves as the 'Children of Huang Di'.

Huang Di inspired many legends of military triumph. He battled Yan Di, a God of Fire, at the plain of Zhuolu (near the Hebei and

Today, the First Emperor is most famous for the extraordinary Terracotta Army, unearthed in 1974 next to his tomb near modern-day Xi'an in Shaanxi Province. Here some 8,000 life-sized clay figures were found buried in pits, portraying soldiers in battle formation, as well as cavalry and some beautiful bronze chariots. These figures have individualized facial features, with many different ethnic identities depicted. More than 600,000 men laboured to build his colossal and, so far, unopened tomb. According to Sima Qian, its underground chambers reproduced the cosmos: the stars and planets were set in pearls in its copper-domed ceiling, and a luxurious palace was surrounded by great rivers and seas reproduced in mercury.

It was Qin Shi Huangdi's administrative acts that were to shape the whole imperial period in China. He built a vast network of roads, created thirty-six provinces with centrally appointed governors, and imposed uniform systems of weights and measures, currency and writing. Yet his acts were not always benevolent. The First Emperor – if we believe Sima Qian's anti-Qin account – also ordered the 'Burning of the Books' in 212 BCE, a fierce campaign to suppress intellectual opposition in which 460 dissenting scholars were buried alive.

A superstitious man, the First Emperor travelled widely, consulting soothsayers and shamans, seeking elixirs that would grant eternal life, and making sacrificial offerings to mountain and river spirits. He sent young men and virgins to contact the immortals in the fabled isles of Penglai across the Eastern Sea (see p. 142). His quest for immortality was to prove in vain: it was on such a trip to the eastern shore that the First Emperor died in 210 BCE.

Shanxi border). They were half-brothers, and each controlled half the world. Huang Di was a compassionate and moral king, but Yan Di was not. This inevitably led to conflict between them. The *Liezi*, a fifth-century BCE Daoist text, reports that Yan Di, fiery ruler that he was, tried to overwhelm his sibling, but Huang Di 'led great bears and brown bears, wolves, leopards, and lesser cats, with tigers in the vanguard; he had for his banners falcons, eagles, and wild pheasants in the air. There were three battles before Huang Di was able to carry out his ambition'. Finally, the Yellow Emperor killed Yan Di and took his lands for his own.

An alternative version of the tale tells us that Huang Di defeated Yan Di but did not kill him; instead, he later reconciled with his half-brother, who by then had many lesser spirits serving under him, and they combined their kingdoms.

Huang Di also battled at Zhuolu with Chiyou, a fierce warrior god. One version of the myth describes how, 'When Huang Di first

---

Xingtian

One of several lesser deities who unsuccessfully challenged Huang Di for supremacy, Xingtian's name, meaning 'Punished by Heaven', reflected his fate. Huang Di cut off his head and buried it on Mount Changyang. Despite this, Xingtian went on fighting; according to the *Shan Hai Jing* ('Classic of Mountains and Seas'), 'he used his nipples as eyes and his navel as mouth. He brandished his shield and axe, and danced'. Although he was defeated, he retained the admiration of the world for not submitting. A poet of the Jin dynasty declared that 'his fierce spirit will live forever'. Xingtian became a symbol of the Chinese people's will to resist whatever difficulties they faced.

Chiyou

Chiyou came from a fearsome family: he had seventy-two brothers, who each like him had a brass head and ate metal and stone. He was said to have invented metal weapons, and so became a powerful god of war. In the *Guanzi*, a collection of mythic texts attributed to the seventh-century BCE official Guan Zong, we learn that Chiyou discovered metal in a mountain spring: 'Then Ge Lu mountain opened up, and there came out water and metal. Chiyou gathered up the metal and fashioned it into swords, armour, spears, and lances. That year he brought under his power nine lords. Then Yong Hu mountain opened up as well, and there came out water and metal. Chiyou gathered up the metal and fashioned it into the lances of Yong Hu and the daggers-axes of Rui.' The dagger-axe was the first Chinese weapon that was designed entirely for battle, rather than hunting, and was used from the Zhou dynasty into the Han period.

The *Shan Hai Jing* ('Classic of Mountains and Seas') gives two accounts of his battle with Huang Di: either he was captured and killed by Huang Di (according to Chapter Seventeen) or the Responding Dragon (Chapter Fourteen). The same book tells us that after he died, the wooden fetters that had been used to bind him turned into a maple grove. The colour red is associated with Chiyou because of the maple tree, and the maple tree remains his symbol among the Miao people of south China, who worship him as a remote ancestor. In Yunnan Province, Miao villages hold an annual festival that involves dancing and blowing reed pipes round a pole adorned with a colourful red flag called 'Chiyou's flag', and because of his horned head and hooves designs of ox horns are embroidered on their clothes and carved on their elaborate silver ornaments.

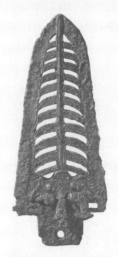

A bronze dagger-axe head dating to 1100–950 CE.

Fengbo and Yushi

The *Shan Hai Jing* ('Classic of Mountains and Seas') records how the God of Wind, Fengbo (*feng* means 'wind' and *bo* means 'lord'), and the God of Rain, Yushi (*yu* means 'rain' and *shi'* means 'master'), unleashed a storm in support of Chiyou in his battle with Huang Di, but were ultimately defeated by the goddess of drought, Ba. Curiously, a different account given by Han Fei Zi, a third-century BCE writer, who portrays Fengbo and Yushi and even Chiyou as deities subordinate to Huang Di rather than his enemies. It describes a procession on Mount Tai: while elephants and dragons pulled Huang Di's cart, Fengbo cleaned the road, Yushi sprinkled water, and Chiyou led the way. Both Fengbo and Yushi gave way later in Chinese legends to the King of Dragons, whom people asked for rain, or to make it cease, in different parts of the country.

established himself, he had to contend with Chiyou. He battled with Chiyou nine times, but did not achieve victory. He had to retreat to Mount Taishan. There was fog for three days and three nights and everything was dark. A woman appeared who had a human head, but the body of a bird. Huang Di prostrated himself to her and did not dare raise his head. The woman said, "I am the Dark Lady. What is it that you want?" Huang Di said, "I would like to gain victory each time I attack, were it ten thousand times, whether as ambush or direct attack, what should I do?" From there he received the strategy of war.'

Huang Di asked the Responding Dragon (see p. 128) to hold back the rain. But Chiyou had command over the gods of wind and rain, Fengbo and Yushi, and ordered them to raise a great tempest. Now Huang Di sought the help of his daughter, Ba, who was the goddess of drought and she stopped the rain, allowing Huang Di to gain victory over Chiyou. For Ba, the story ends less happily: after helping her father, she could not return to heaven, and wherever on earth she stayed was afflicted by terrible drought. Huang Di commanded her to live north of the Red River, but she often fled from there, taking drought with her. Only by dredging canals and praying to her to 'go north to where you should stay' could people restore the rain. In pre-Communist times, before Mao Zedong initiated the construction of various dams including the great Three Gorges Dam, there were a myriad of rituals in rural China to drive Ba away and bring rain to help the farmers.

The *Shan Hai Jing* also tells us how Huang Di killed the one-legged monster Kui, and used his hide to make a drum which sounded so loud that all the world stood in awe: 'Its shape was like a bull, dark grey was his body, with no horns on his head, and only one foot. When it emerged from the sea it was always accompanied by a tempest. Its eyes were bright like the sun and moon. Its voice

Kui

The *Shan Hai Jing* ('Classic of Mountains and Seas') describes Kui as a strange, somewhat ominous beast. However, a number of early sources tell us that Kui was a master of music for the Sage Kings Yao and Shun. He invented song by imitating the sounds he heard in mountain forests; if he beat on a stone, every creature would follow his melody and dance.

Confucius made a pun out of Kui's one leggedness: *Kui yi zu* meant either 'one foot Kui' or 'one person like Kui is enough' (*zu* can mean 'foot' or 'enough').

was like thunder. Its name was Kui. Huang Di has captured it and made its skin into a drum. When he struck it with a bone from the Thunder God, the noise reverberated over five hundred *li* (one *li* is half a kilometre or a third of a mile) and caused the world to submit.' Although Chiyou could fly in the air and run the steepest of paths, when Huang Di struck his Kui drum, Chiyou was stopped in his tracks and Huang Di beheaded him.

Huang Di's inventions

Huang Di was said to have invented many things useful to humans, among them the *zhinan* ('south-pointing chariot'), a lodestone, or naturally magnetized piece of the mineral magnetite, that pointed to the south. We have examples of these from the Han dynasty, though they were not used until many centuries later for navigation. Instead, they were used to align houses, crops and tombs to the desired cardinal directions.

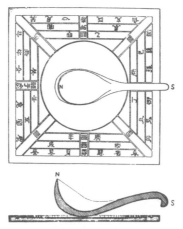

Drawing of an ancient Chinese *zhinan*, a lodestone compass,
said to have been invented by Huang Di.

According to a Han-dynasty inscription next to a carving depicting Huang Di, he 'invented weapons and the well-and-field system'. (The form in which the Chinese organized the land, was in the shape of the character for 'well', 井, leaving the central space for the upkeep of the ancestral shrine and other social aspects that benefited the widows and orphans of the clan.) Apparently Huang Di also devised 'upper and lower garments, and established palaces and houses', and it was at his instigation that his advisor Cangjie invented writing.

Huang Di's consort, Leizu, is also credited as an inventor of sericulture (silk production), which is known to have originated in China. Archaeological evidence of silk has been found dating as early the fourth millennium BCE, and by the Zhou era (*c.* 1046–256 BCE) it

Silk production is shown in the Qing-dynasty *Yuzhi gengzhi tu* ('Imperially Commissioned Illustrations of Agriculture and Sericulture').

seems to have been quite widely available. However, sericulture was a mainly female occupation, and female activities were excluded from written sources by the (predominantly male) scribal class. Yet Sima Qian tells us that Huang Di married as his first and chief consort Leizu, who in many sources was the original silkworm goddess, and she is still worshipped as such. She was said to have been born on the fifteenth day of the third month of the lunar calendar. On this

---

Cangjie: Inventor of Chinese Writing

In the texts of the Warring States period (476–221 BCE), we find many brief references to Cangjie. He was the official historian to Huang Di, who was dissatisfied with the rope knotting method of writing, the only system then in existence (early Tibetans kept notes by knotting string). So Cangjie sat down beside a river to think of a better way to record events and things, and saw a unique footprint that had been left by a phoenix. Wondering what could have made the print, he asked a huntsman, who told him that each bird had a characteristic footprint. This gave Cangjie his idea: he set out to discover the unique characteristics of each object and turn them into pictograms, forming a writing system. He presented the emperor with his findings. Huang Di was delighted and spread knowledge of it all over the empire. So much so that during the night even ghosts cried, for they were afraid that they could be accused of crimes by men's writing.

Since the Chinese writing system is very complicated, and until the twentieth century was the prerogative of an upper class that closely guarded the skill, it is not surprising that a mythical god should have been thought to have invented it. To the common people, the ability to read and write was almost holy, and many shrines to Cangjie survive in China to this day. Cangjie is still honoured in the 'Cangjie input method', a way of typing Chinese characters (based on stroke order) using a QWERTY keyboard. This method is still commonly used in Taiwan, but it is complicated, and most

---

day, a large sacrificial ceremony is held near Leizu Village, which still continues to this day. It is appropriate for Leizu to be so honoured in Sichuan, since Sichuan is long famed for sericulture.

There had been many other versions of the silkworm god. One of them goes by the name of Cancong: '*can*' means 'silkworm' and '*cong*' means 'a cluster'. It is a name that has been found in texts describing the god or kings of Shu (ancient Sichuan). Written evidence

people instead input characters by their pronunciation in the Mandarin dialect Standard Chinese – known in China as the *guoyu* ('national language') or *putonghua* ('common tongue') – established in the twentieth century. Standard Chinese is now the official language of China, but there remain eight primary (and mutually unintelligible) dialects and hundreds of local variations of these.

A Qing-dynasty illustration of Cangjie, inventor of the Chinese writing system.

comes from a Tang-dynasty text, citing earlier sources that have now been lost.

> Cancong set himself up as King of Shu. According to tradition, he taught the people about silkworms and mulberry. He made several thousand golden silkworms. At the start of each year, he took the golden silkworms and gave the people one silkworm each. The silkworms the people raised always multiplied prolifically, so that in the end they could return the gift to the king. When he went on a royal tour of his realm, wherever he stopped on his journey, the people created a market town. Because of his legacy people in Shu hold a silkworm market every spring.

Another legend of the silkworm is told in the fourth-century CE *Soushen Ji* ('In Search of the Supernatural'). It must have been well-known to people through the oral tradition, or its author, Gan Bao, would not have said at the beginning: *jiu shuo*, 'Of old it was said...'.

> Of old it was said that in ancient times there was a man who had to make a long journey for military service; there was no one left at home, only a daughter. They had a stallion, whom the girl was feeding. There was no one around when she thought of her father, and said playfully to the horse, 'If you could make my father return, I will marry you.' When the horse heard this, he broke his bridle and set off. After many miles he arrived at where the father was. The father was both pleased and surprised at seeing the horse, took it and rode it. When the horse

saw him come, he whinnied and kept looking sadly at the place from where he had come. The father said, 'This horse has no reason to behave like this, has someone in my family died?' He rode it and returned home.

There the horse seemed to have shown such intelligence that the father gave it extra feed, but the horse would not eat. Whenever the horse saw the daughter, it became excited and animated. The father thought it very strange and secretly asked his daughter. She told her father everything, and he thought that her offer of marriage must be the reason. The father said, 'Do not say anything, I am afraid that you might bring shame upon our house, but don't go out'. The father killed the horse with an arrow from his crossbow, skinned it, and left the skin to dry in the courtyard. The father went out, leaving his daughter to play with a neighbour's daughter near the horse's skin. She kicked it, saying, 'You are an animal, and you wanted to marry a human for a wife. Because of this you have been skinned, now what is the point of that?' She had hardly stopped speaking, when suddenly the horse's skin rose up and wrapped itself around her. The neighbour's girl was very scared and went and told the father, but it was too late. Several days later, in between the branches of a large tree, the girl with the horse's skin had turned completely into a silkworm, spinning itself into a cocoon…. Because of this story, people named the tree the *sang* tree, *sang* meaning *lost*. Everyone now cultivates this kind of tree…. The ritual in Han times was that the empress herself collected mulberry leaves and sacrificed to the God of Sericulture [Cancong].

YAN DI

Yan Di (the 'fire' or 'flame' god) was the half-brother of Huang Di, to whom he lost the battle for world dominance. In early texts he was recognized as one of the Five August Emperors (see box, p. 45), ruling the summer season and the south with his subordinate Zhuming. In later tradition he was revered, like Huang Di, as an ancestor of the Chinese people.

One poignant myth in the *Shan Hai Jing* ('Classic of Mountains and Seas') concerns Yan Di's daughter, Nu Wa (not to be confused with Nuwa, the creator goddess; the character employed for '*wa*' is different, and means 'child or daughter'). The story goes that Nu Wa 'was playing in the east sea when she sank and drowned. So she became the Jingwei. (A *jingwei* is a mythical bird or spirit

Nu Wa is transformed into the mythical Jingwei.
From a Ming-dynasty edition of the *Shan Hai Jing*.

guardian.) She carries in her beak pieces of wood and pebbles to throw into the [water] in the hope that she can dam the vast east sea.' Just as her father was overcome by the superior Huang Di, so she is drowned by the powerful forces of the sea, but she takes her revenge by attempting to dam it.

In other mythic traditions, Yan Di has two significant descendants: Chiyou, the God of War (see p. 87), and Zhurong, the God of Fire (see p. 103).

DI JUN

The first mention of Di (or Emperor) Jun is in the *Shan Hai Jing*, probably composed in the first century CE. Here he is a major deity and ancestor of culture-bearing descendants. Scholars speculate that he was the chief god of the Yin people in East China, just as Huang Di was the chief god of the Xia people of West China. Thus when the Yin kingdom collapsed, Di Jun's myth faded.

Di Jun features most prominently in the solar and lunar myths connected with his consorts Xihe and Changxi, and the exploits of Yi the Archer and his disobedient wife, Chang'e: 'Di Jun give Yi the vermilion bow and white stringed arrows, and told him to aid the people in the kingdom below. Yi did this to help the people below with their hundreds of hardships.'

The *Shan Hai Jing* tells us that all eight of Di Jun's sons were associated with musical instruments, singing and dancing. In the same chapter we are also told that 'Emperor Jun gave birth to Yanlong. It was Yanlong who created the lute and the zither'. Quite clearly there were many mythic traditions, attributing the creation of different aspects of culture to a variety of different gods or heroes. Di Jun's most famous and divine son was Houji, the millet god (see p. 74).

There is another shadowy but high-status deity Di (or Emperor) Ku, also known by the name of Gaoxin. He may well have been another version of Di Jun, as he is said to have had some of the same wives and sons. He was a grandson of Huang Di and sometimes named as one of the Five August Emperors. His main significance, apart from his association with several musical instruments and songs, seems to have been his role as an ancestor god. He was the consort of two goddesses, Jian Di and Jiang Yuan, who each bore a son by virgin birth. These sons, Qi (or Xie) and Houji, became legendary rulers of the Shang and Zhou dynasties respectively. Di Ku features as a chief god (as Gaoxin) in a pre-Han dynasty myth about two quarrelling brothers, whom Gaoxin sought to divide by making them masters of two separate stars, Shen and Chen (see p. 62). Gaoxin again crops up in the much later, post-Han story of Panhu the divine dog (not to be confused with Pangu, the giant) as ancestor to the so-called Man Barbarians. The story, related in the fourth-century CE *Soushen Ji* ('In Search of the Supernatural'), states explicitly that it aims to explain the uncivilized nature of the 'barbarians', whose origins, it claims, lay in a bestial union between man and beast:

> In the time of Gaoxin a physician made a pet of a strange dog that had hatched from an insect-like creature that had given an old woman severe earache. This dog had been placed in a gourd (*hu*) covered by a plate (*pan*) and so he got the name of Panhu. It happened that the king of the country [Gaoxin] was troubled by a rebellion, and said,

A brick-rubbing of the Emperor Ku, one of the
mythical Five August Emperors of the Han dynasty.

'Whoever gets rid of this rebellion will be rewarded with
a lot of gold and land, as well as the hand of my youngest
daughter!' On hearing this the dog departed; sometime
later it brought back in its jaws the head of the rebels'
commander, at which the rebellion collapsed. The king
was very glad, but he could not reward the dog as he had
promised: 'Panhu is an animal, he cannot be rewarded
with the princess as a bride.' Whereupon Gaoxin's daughter
came forward, and entreated the king to honour his pledge,
'made before the whole world', lest he bring catastrophe
on his kingdom. The king acquiesced, and Panhu led the
princess as his wife up the South Mountain. Several years

passed and Panhu died. The princess returned to court with the children whom the dog had fathered. This is the origin of the Man Barbarians, who having lived in the wild could not get used to civilization.

There are several other versions of this story; in one, Panhu is offered a chance to turn into a human by enclosing himself in an upturned bell, but the king cannot help but peep in before the transformation is complete. The dog had turned into a human except for his head, so the princess is obliged to don a dog-mask in imitation of her husband.

SHAOHAO

Shaohao was undoubtedly one of the chief gods – he is sometimes given as one of the Five August Emperors – yet our sources are somewhat conflicting. The ancient *Huainanzi*, in its account of the Five Directions, associates Shaohao with the west (see p. 26), where he supposedly founded his capital. In Chapter Two of the *Shan Hai Jing* ('Classic of Mountains and Seas') we learn that Shaohao lived on a western mountain named Changliu, inhabited by 'wild beasts with spotted tails and birds with spotted heads', and from here he observed the condition of the sunset. However, another chapter from the *Shan Hai Jing* not only links him with the east but also with Zhuanxu (p. 104): 'Beyond the Eastern Sea there is a great pool where Shaohao had his kingdom. Shaohao had the God Zhuanxu suckled here, and he threw away his lute and zither.' The *Zuo Zhuan* ('Zuo Tradition'), a narrative history compiled in the fourth century BCE,

A Qing-dynasty print of a nine-headed phoenix,
with the tail feathers of a peacock.

reports, 'When Shaohao came to the throne, phoenix birds suddenly appeared. He therefore took the birds as his emblem, creating a bird minister and birds for official titles'. This is a recurring pattern in classical Chinese mythology. Phoenixes, composite birds with the head of a pheasant, wings of a swallow, beak of a parrot, legs of a crane and body of a duck, appeared auspiciously at moments of happiness and glory. They later came to symbolize the empress, just as the dragon symbolized the emperor.

The Han historian Sima Qian, who was the first to attempt to transform Huang Di into a historical figure and founder of the Chinese race, makes no mention of Shaohao. Gu Jiegang (see p. 11) believed that Shaohao was inserted between Huang Di and Zhuanxu by the imperial librarian Liu Xin (*c.* 50 BCE–23 CE) as part of his editing of ancient texts in order to create a narrative that would legitimize the rule of the Han dynasty.

In the *Shiyi Ji* ('Records of Forgotten Tales'), compiled by the fourth-century CE scholar Wang Jia, Shaohao was the son of Huang'e, a weaver goddess who fell in love with the planet Venus. Shaohao's tomb, sited in the east of Qufu (Confucius' birthplace) in Shandong Province, has a temple to him, probably built in the Song dynasty.

GONGGONG

Not all of the great gods were benign. The rebellious Gonggong, a serpentine water god, was often blamed for unleashing great floods on China. (We will return to the recurrence of floods in Chinese mythology in Chapter Six.) From the *Huainanzi* we learn that, 'In the time of Shun, Gonggong stirred up the floodwaters so that it drowned the furthest south, the area round the Hollow Mulberry.' A story probably composed in the fifth century BCE and preserved in the *Guoyu* ('Discourses of the States') gives a slightly different account: '[Gonggong] wanted to dam the hundred rivers, reduce the highest ground, and block up the low-lying ground, and so he damaged the world. But August Heaven opposed his good fortune and the common people refused to help him. Disaster and disorder sprang up everywhere and Gonggong was destroyed.'

The orthodox version of the myth changed to involve Gonggong as a mighty warrior who challenged the sky god Zhuanxu for supremacy: 'Long ago, Gonggong fought with Zhuanxu to be chief of the

Zhurong: God of Fire

According to Chapter Eighteen of *Shan Hai Jing* ('Classic of Mountains and Seas'), Zhurong was descended from the God of Flame, Yan Di (see p. 96). Perhaps appropriately, both were seen as principal gods of fire; in fact, *zhurong* is still an alternative word for 'fire', and China's first rover to land on another planet was named Zhurong and sent to Mars – *huoxing*, 'planet of fire'.

Zhurong's high status is signified by his inclusion in some texts as one of the Three Divine Sovereigns (see p. 76). In the *Shan Hai Jing*, we are told that, 'In the south was Zhurong, who had the body of a beast, but a human face, and he rode on two dragons'. In some stories Zhurong fights the God of Water, Gonggong, and wins. As in the myth involving Gonggong's conflict with Zhuanxu, Gonggong bumps into the Mount Buzhou, which was situated in the great sea. The *Shan Hai Jing* also tells us that Zhurong is the one who kills Gun, who stole the magical *xirang* ('growing soil) in his attempt to quell the flood (see p. 113).

gods. In his fury he knocked against Mount Buzhou. The pillar of heaven broke and the chord of earth snapped. Heaven tilted towards the northwest, and that is why the sun, moon and stars move in that direction. Earth has a gap missing the southeast, and that is why the rivers overflowed and silt and soil came to rest there.' As we have seen, the ancestral goddess Nuwa then mended the sky with her five-coloured stones (p. 66). Some versions of this myth describe how he fought Di Ku or the fire god Zhurong instead of Zhuanxu.

ZHUANXU

Zhuanxu, one of the Five August Emperors (see p. 45), was the grandson and successor of Huang Di. Although Zhuanxu, also known as Gaoyang, was one of the most important gods, we know little of him from the written sources.

Zhuanxu had many sons, and for a god who was mostly benign, it is notable that his sons were not; some were plague ghosts, others terrible beasts. He also had two grandsons, Zhong and Li, whom he ordered to separate heaven and earth. Zhong used all his strength to support the heavens with his two hands while Li, likewise, held the earth down with his two hands. So the two kept heaven and earth apart, according to the *Shan Hai Jing*.

Another version explains that the Supreme God instructed Zhong and Li in this way: 'Ordinary people lost their trust, society was chaotic... at the same time he ordered Zhong to keep the way of the gods, and Li to take care of the people, and both to return to the old order .... He ordered Zhong and Li to break the path by which

---

Worship of Zhuanxu

According to the *Shan Hai Jing* ('Classic of Mountains and Seas'), Zhuanxu was buried at Mount Wuyu in northern Fujian Province with his nine concubines, though today many places in the provinces of Henan, Hebei and Shandong claim to be home to the great god's tomb. Every March in Neihuang County, Henan Province, a festival is held to celebrate his birth, attended by pilgrims from far and wide. He is worshipped as one of the originators of humanity.

---

heaven and earth were open to each other.' From then on, men and gods were separated from each other, and no more could the gods create havoc amongst men. This account appears in the *Shang Shu* ('Book of Documents'), probably as a product of the Western Zhou, that pre-dates the Han-dynasty sources.

LINGLUN: GOD OF MUSIC

Many myths recount the invention of music and musical instruments, and many gods were credited with their creation. In the *Lushi Chunqiu* ('Master Lu's Annals of Spring and Autumn'), a Qin-dynasty text allegedly written around 239 BCE under the chancellor Lu Buwei, it is said that: '[Di] Ku … ordered Youchui to make the war drum, the bells, the chimes, the panpipes … [Di] Ku commanded people to play them. Some beat on the drums … some blew on the panpipes, some performed on the flutes so that they made the phoenix dance. [Di] Ku was very pleased.' The most popular creator of music, however, was the culture hero Linglun, who was said to be

A late seventh-century earthenware group of female musicians clapping and playing the *tongba* (small copper cymbals), *konghou* (harp), and *pipa* (lute).

Huang Di's governor of music. In later tradition, he was respected as the God of Music and the divine ancestor of actors: to this day actors are called *lingren*, 'people of Linglun'.

Linglun crafted a pipe out of a piece of bamboo, whose sound created the five notes of the Chinese five-tone scale (equivalent to *do*, *re*, *mi*, *so* and *la* in the western *solfeggio* system). And he created the eight sounds made by eight musical instruments, including the bell, string drum, and two percussion and the three wind instruments.

~~~~~

DEMIGODS AND HEROES
OF THE CLASSICAL ERA

The most important of the demigods (or heroes) in the classical era were the Three Sage Kings: most commonly Yao, Shun and Yu, although Huang Di also appears among their number in some sources. Texts from the Zhou dynasty (1046–256 BCE) describe the period of their rule as a golden age and the Han-dynasty scholar Sima Qian begins his account of the ancient history of China with the Emperor Yao. We have many more sources to draw on when reconstructing the myths and legends surrounding these individuals, as they fit in well with Confucianist thinking, emulating the proper moral behaviour of Confucius' mandate of heaven.

YAO

According to the myths, Yao was a man of perfect virtue. In the first book, 'Basic Annals of the Five Emperors', of the *Shiji*, Sima Qian says: '[Yao's] benevolence was that of heaven. His intelligence was that of the spirits … he was rich, yet not arrogant, noble, yet not contemptuous of others.' Yao was praised by Confucianists as the exemplar of kingship, who kept things running in perfect order. He even handed on his throne to one who was worthy of it, rather than to his own son, a supreme act of wisdom.

Weiqi, or the game of Go

Weiqi (literally 'encirclement boardgame'), invented in China and known as 'Go' in Japanese and the western world, was called *Yi* in the earliest textual references to it from the fourth century BCE. *Weiqi* is a strategy game for two players: the aim is to surround more territory on the board than one's opponent. Originally played on a 17-by-17-line grid, since the Tang dynasty it has used a 19-by-19-line grid. It has relatively simple rules, but in reality is very complex – it is estimated that the number of possible games exceeds the number of atoms in the known universe.

Weiqi was considered one of the four cultivated arts of the Chinese scholar-gentleman, together with calligraphy, painting and playing the *guqin* (an ancient zither).

Men playing a game of *weiqi* in imperial China,
probably Ming dynasty.

Yao had a miraculous birth: his mother, Qingdu, who came to be worshipped as the Mother of Yao, was visited by a Red Dragon, which descended on her while she was sitting by a river. She gave birth fourteen months later. Thus, while Yao was allegedly the son of Di Ku or Di Jun – divine spouse of Qingdu – he was actually the son of this Red Dragon. He lived with his mother's parents until he was ten years old.

As the emperor's son, at the age of twenty Yao became ruler of China. He is credited with establishing the system of dividing the year into seasons, and creating a calendrical count that is still with us as the lunar calendar. He also reputedly instituted many rituals that were still observed until the end of the imperial age.

A Song-dynasty scroll painting of the Emperor Yao, one of the Five Emperors.

Yao's eldest son, Dan Zhu, was fond of gaming and so Yao invented *weiqi* (see box p. 108), which he taught to his son. Indeed, Dan Zhu's skill at the game surpassed all others. Yet Yao thought Dan Zhu too frivolous to rule the world well, and instead passed his throne to a man he felt worthy, called Shun. Yao exiled his eldest son; some versions even have Yao execute him. After Yao's death, Shun tried to cede the throne to Dan Zhu, but the people would not hear of it. So Shun became the ruler, until he in turn passed the throne not to his eldest son but to someone unrelated to him: Yu.

Yao reigned for over seventy years before being succeeded by Shun, and then survived for another twenty-eight years, dying aged 119. Yao's significance for Confucianists may lie not only in his wise choice of a suitable successor, but also his role in enlisting Yi the Archer to save humanity from drought (see p. 54) and – according to some versions – his part in Gun and Yu's conquest of the terrible floods (see p. 113).

SHUN

Shun was Yao's successor. He lost his mother at a young age, and his father, the Blind Old Man, married another woman. She had an arrogant son named Xiang ('Elephant') on account of his big nose. The Blind Old Man loved his second wife and thought often of getting rid of Shun. Despite their cruelty, Shun treated his father and step-brother with love and great respect, and he was well-known for his filial piety (a great Chinese virtue, according to Confucius) by the time he was twenty years old. When he was thirty, he was recommended to Emperor Yao as a suitable successor.

A Qing-dynasty illustration of the legendary
Emperor Shun, last of the Five Emperors.

Yao ordered his two daughters, Ehuang and Nuying (see p. 136)
to marry Shun, and asked his nine sons to befriend him so that
they could observe his behaviour. Yao gave Shun fine linen to wear,
and a zither to play on; warehouses were built for him and he was
given oxen and sheep.

The Blind Old Man and his son tried to murder Shun. First, the
Blind Old Man ordered him to repair the roof of a barn. When
Shun told his two wives, Ehuang and Nuying, they said, 'Be careful,
they might harm you; they might set fire to the roof. Take off your
old coat and put this one on with its bird patterns.' When Shun had
climbed to the top of the roof, his father took away the ladder and

set the barn on fire, just as Ehuang and Nuying had predicted. But Shun flew down in his magic coat. Another time, the Blind Old Man asked Shun to dredge a well. Again Shun told his two wives, and they said, 'Be careful, they might harm you. Take off your coat and put this on with its dragon patterns.' Shun went to dredge the well, and his father and step-brother blocked the opening to the well and so it filled up; but Shun escaped by swimming away, assisted by his magical robes. Finally, the Blind Old Man tried to get Shun drunk and kill him, but his wives had put Shun in a bath with a magic lotion that prevented drunkenness, even after drinking all day.

The Blind Old Man and Xiang, believing that Shun was dead, divided up his possessions. The son wanted Yao's two daughters and Shun's zither, while the father took the oxen, the sheep, and the warehouses. Xiang was in Shun's house, playing on his zither, just as Shun walked in. Xiang was surprised and said 'I was thinking of you and felt very sad.' Shun said 'Indeed! You are behaving as you ought to.' Shun – the exemplar of filial piety – went on serving his father, but treated his step-brother with newfound circumspection.

Yao had a further trial for Shun: Shun was sent to a forest in the mountains. Through squalls and thunderstorms, he did not lose his way. Yao then knew that Shun was worthy enough to be given the world. Shun ruled well and wisely. He died when on an inspection of his southern kingdom and was buried 'in the wilds of Cangwu', possibly in Hunan Province.

Shun's widows, Ehuang and Nuying, went to visit his grave. According to local legend, they wept on the bamboo trees by the Xiang River (a tributary of the Yangtze), making them grow forevermore with the stains of the goddesses' tears. This is the origin of the spotted bamboo that is used for decorative furniture in China, which thereafter was called the Bamboo of the Goddesses of Xiang, or *Xiangfei zhu*. The goddesses themselves supposedly drowned in the Xiang River, where a tempest blew up while they were visiting Shun's grave. They have thus become the Goddesses of the Xiang River (see p. 136).

Shun's successor was Yu, who received his throne in the same way as Shun had received his from Yao. Just as Yi the Archer had saved the world from scorching drought, so the beneficent demigods Gun and his son, Yu, would tame the flood that devastated China.

GUN AND YU TAME THE WATERS

We read of Yu in the very earliest of our written sources. Many such references are fragmentary, but they all point to his importance: he is called Da ('Great') Yu. Yu was favoured by the gods and had many supernatural helpers in his mission to stop a great deluge, which was forcing people to flee to the mountains. He worked so hard to protect the people that 'three times he passed his own house but did not go in', a saying that has entered colloquial speech, referring to those who work tirelessly with no thought of their own comfort. He is said to have lived under the kingship of Shun, second of the Three Sage Kings (see p. 110), whom he then succeeded, founding the legendary first dynasty of China: the Xia.

Gun

Yu was carrying out a duty once assigned to his father, Gun. The *Shan Hai Jing* ('Classic of Mountains and Seas') tells us that the Supreme God (some other sources say the Emperor Yao) asked the other gods who should be put in charge of stopping the flood, and they recommended Gun. Although the Supreme God did not like him, he nonetheless gave him the task (according to the *Tian Wen*). For nine years, Gun struggled against the rising water, even attempting to block it with magical earth that he had stolen from the Supreme God. This earth, called *xirang* ('growing soil'), swelled up by itself and thus kept the waters at bay.

When the Supreme God found out that Gun had stolen his *xirang*, he became very angry and ordered the God of Fire, Zhurong, to kill Gun near Yushan ('Feather Mountain'). Gun was duly executed, but his body did not decay. After three years, his belly was opened up to reveal his son, Yu. The Supreme God now ordered Yu to carry out the task that Gun had failed to complete. This time, Yu asked for permission to use the *xirang*, and the Supreme God granted it.

Yu

The *Tian Wen* ('Heavenly Questions') gives us tantalizing glimpses of the outline of this story: 'How did he fill the flood waters up at their deepest? How did he set bounds to the Nine Provinces of the earth? What did the winged dragon trace on the ground? Where did the seas and rivers flow?' Rather than attempt to block off the flood at a single point, Yu channelled the water into nine rivers. The Responding Dragon (see p. 128), one of Yu's supernatural helpers, beat the land with its tail, marking out the rivers that would control the water. The *Shang Shu* ('Book of Documents'), one of the Five Classics allegedly collected by Confucius, tells us the outcome of Yu's efforts: 'The grounds along the Nine Provinces were made habitable; the Nine Mountains were cleared of superfluous woods; the sources of the Nine Rivers were opened up; the Nine Marshes

A Qing-dynasty porcelain plate
depicting a dragon and carp.

were banked; access to the capital was secured within the Four Seas. The Six Treasuries were repaired; comparisons were made between the areas so that revenues were adjusted; the fields were classified according to their soil. Yu set an example of virtue, and none would act contrary to his conduct.'

At Dragon Gate, at the east end of the Yellow River, Yu made a cave that was about one *li* (half a kilometre or a third of a mile) long. The river rushed through this opening; there was room for neither horses nor for people on either side. Every year, in the spring, yellow carp from the sea and all the islands would arrive at Dragon Gate, but only seventy-two carp were allowed to pass through to Dragon Gate Cave. Upon crossing the threshold, clouds and rain gathered, and fire from the sky burned off their tails; thus, they turned into dragons. This episode has survived in colloquial speech today, when people talk about how 'the carp turn into dragons', referring to candidates who pass the Civil Service Examinations with honours.

Another version of Yu's achievements, from the *Shizi* (fourth century BCE), recounts: 'In ancient times the Dragon Gate had not been opened... its waters were swollen and its current irregular, so that it destroyed all in its path, and this became known as the Flood. Yu channelled the river and sluiced it. For ten years Yu did not visit his home, the nails stopped growing on his hands, no hair grew on his legs. He was afflicted with an illness that made his body shrivel, so that when he walked he could not lift one leg past the other; people called it "the Yu walk".'

As well as the flood itself, Yu had to eliminate the monsters that it had brought forth. One of these creatures was Xiangliu, who the *Shan Hai Jing* ('Classic of Mountains and Seas') tells us was 'a subordinate of Gonggong. He was a snake with nine heads with a voracious appetite. He whirled round and ate whatever was on the myriad hills. Whatever he touched turned to bog, with the water being either sour or bitter so that none of the animals could live. Yu blocked the flooding water and killed Xiangliu; its blood contaminated the land so that the people could not grow any crops on it. The area was too full of water for people to live there. Yu tried to fill the area, but three times the land collapsed. Yu had no alternative but to make it a mighty pool of water, and with the help of all the gods they built a platform, which is to the north of Mount Kunlun.'

The *Wu Yue Chunqiu* ('Spring and Autumn Annals of Wu and Yue'), compiled by Zhao Yue, a historian of the Eastern Han dynasty (25–220 CE), and probably based on texts written in the first century BCE, tells us how Yu found a wife. He was getting on in years, and lonely. So he prayed for a sign, and one day he saw a white fox with nine tails. He followed it, remembering a folksong that promised good fortune to anyone who married a girl from Tushan: 'Yu said, "White is the colour of my robes, and nine tails are the symbols of a king. A song of Tushan goes,

> A white fox seeks a mate
> His nine tails are bushy and strong.
> My house honours guests (?).
> My guest will be king,
> My house will flourish, my clan too,
> I will make you flourish.
> Heaven and mankind unite in this,
> I must not delay.

"Now I understand."' Yu then married a girl from Tushan, and called her Nujiao ('Beautiful Girl').

Yan Shiku (581–645 BCE) continues the story in a no longer extant passage of the *Huainanzi*: 'While Yu was making the channels for the water, he turned into a bear in order to get a greater purchase on the stones. He had told the Tushan Girl, who was bringing food to him, that he would beat on a stone drum when it was time for her to come. When he was at his task, he accidentally drummed on a stone. When the Tushan Girl heard this, she thought it was the arranged signal to bring him food, but fled in fright and horror at the sight of the bear. Yu chased after her till she turned to stone. Then he cried out, "Give me back my son", for when she fled she was heavily pregnant. The stone split open and his son, Qi, was born. The name means "Open".'

Yu took nine years to successfully conquer the waters, and then he commanded Tai Zhang, one of his ministers, to measure the land. From the east pole to the west, it measured 233,575 paces. He commanded another minister, Shu Hai, to measure 233,575 paces from the north pole to the south. Finally, from the deepest abyss of the flood, above twenty-four feet, Yu measured 233,559 paces. Then Yu damned the flood waters with the Supreme God's magical *xirang*, and thus created the mountains. In this way he created the Nine Provinces of China. The Nine Provinces was a term used to designate the area controlled by the Shang dynasty, but as more areas were brought under Chinese control in the Zhou and later, the term became obsolete by the Three Kingdoms period.

Having established the land of China, Yu travelled to more distant regions, largely in search of knowledgeable souls who might help

---

The Nine Tripod Cauldrons

Yu was also believed to have cast the Nine Tripod Cauldrons. These elaborate cauldrons, or *ding*, were made of gold that had been amassed as tribute from the Nine Provinces. According to the *Zuo Zhuan* ('Zuo Tradition') they were carved with 'pictures and signs that showed people which were the good and bad supernatural beings, so that people would know what to do if they encountered malign demons on their travels into watery lands or into forests'. These cauldrons came to symbolize imperial power as they passed from the Xia dynasty down to the Qin. They also cast judgment on rulers and their regimes, growing heavier when the government was virtuous and lighter when it was not, thus pronouncing the mandate of heaven. Sadly, they were lost during the wars of conquest in the late second century BC and though the First Emperor sent a thousand men to search for them, they were never recovered.

Fangfeng the Giant

Apart from his flood-taming activities, Yu was also known as an exorcist who drove out demons. Another minor god encountered by the hero Yu was Fangfeng the giant. The *Guoyu* ('Discourses of the States') records a late Zhou-dynasty text of the fifth century BCE attributed to Confucius: 'Long ago, Yu assembled all the gods on Mount Guiji [in modern Zhejiang Province]. Fangfeng arrived too late. Yu had him killed and beheaded his corpse. One bone of his skeleton filled an entire cart because it was so large.'

According to the *Shiyi Ji*, compiled nearly a thousand years later in the fourth century CE, there was a temple to Fangfeng in eastern China in which his figure was portrayed with a dragon head and ox ears. By contrast, legends collected in the 1980s depict him as a culture hero who tried to control the flood, but was wrongly killed by Yu.

the Chinese people extend the use of their fields. We learn of the lands Yu visited from pseudo-geographical books. For instance, the *Lushi Chunqiu* ('Master Lu's Annals of Spring and Autumn'), compiled around 139 BCE, tells us of his trip to 'the land where people had Black Teeth'. The *Shan Hai Jing* ('Classic of Mountains and Seas') mentions one place where people had holes exposed in their breasts, and another where people had only one arm but three eyes. Most of these places are obviously mythical, but some are still recognizable, especially those containing the names of rivers. Many of these places were great objects of Chinese curiosity. Those that have been tentatively identified include the silk-producing area of Sichuan and Dunhuang in the far northwest, as well as areas on China's borders such as Korea, Khotan and India, 'the land of sky-poison'.

Yu exemplified good Confucian leadership. He was a figure with godlike power, who controlled the flood and saved humanity. He was a courageous warrior who fought off fierce monsters. He mapped out the world and created the Nine Cauldrons that weighed good government in the balance. He put public duty before private concerns. Almost all of the sources that tell us his stories belong to the Zhou dynasty, although he still appears in texts composed much later. And despite his mythical status, he was accorded 'human status' in that his tomb was near Shaoxing, a significant site visited by the First Emperor, Qin Shi Huangdi in 210 BC and where he is still venerated.

LEGENDARY METALSMITHS

After Huang Di and Yan Di battled for supremacy over the world, Huang Di battled against Chiyou, the God of War, on the plain of Zhuolu. It is not surprising that the makers of weapons had a special place in people's minds, especially during the Warring States period (476–221 BCE). Chiyou, as we have seen, was famed for his skill in crafting weaponry, and archaeology has shown us that such creations were not entirely the preserve of fantasy. Some of the bronze instruments, such as the Sword of Goujian recovered from an ancient Chu capital and probably made around 550 BCE, exhibit clearly the remarkable skill of their makers. The famous swordsmiths of mythology, such as Mo Ye and her husband Gan Jiang, were allegedly active during the Warring States period.

Another legendary figure, Ou Yezi, is said to be the ancestor of all smiths. Most smiths would have made bronze swords that were in common use, but as we learn from the ancient stories they did experiment with iron, a technology most scholars agree came from the Middle East. It was Ou Yezi who discovered that iron could be used to make swords, and many named swords were said to have been made by his hand. One source names Ou Yezi as being the father of Mo Ye, and so father-in-law to Gan Jiang. Another source tells us that Gan Jiang was taught by the same master as Ou Yezi.

The *Wu Yue Chunqiu* ('Spring and Autumn Annals of Wu and Yue') tells the story of Gan Jiang and Mo Ye, the most popular account of mythical swordsmithing. The book is sadly no longer extant, but it is quoted in later works. Wu and Yue were kingdoms of the Warring States period, and famous for having the best craftsmen in all of China. The story shows the hard work of the smiths who made the named swords and whose reputations spread throughout the Chinese world. They often made two swords at the same time, the male and the female; and human sacrifice was often demanded. The story also shows the amount of lore that had already attached itself to the making of iron swords.

> Gan Jiang was a man of Wu. He once shared the same
> master as Ou Yezi did formerly; both were good at making
> swords. The Kingdom of Yue sent Wu a gift of three
> swords, which the king of Wu, He Lu, greatly prized. So he
> made the craftsmen make two swords: one to be called
> Gan Jiang, the other Mo Ye, for Mo Ye was the wife of

The bronze sword of King Bu Guang of Yue, Warring States period.

Gan Jiang. When Gan Jiang made the sword, he took the best ore from mines of the five famous mountains. He waited for the best times, watched for the shape of the land, when the Yin and Yang were right, and the myriad gods could be present and observe.

Although the temperature reduced, the best of metals that they had gathered did not fuse together. Gan Jiang did not know the reason. Mo Ye asked him, 'Your good reputation as a swordsmith has reached the king, so he commanded you to make the sword. If it is not completed within three months, what is the reason for it?' Gan Jiang said, 'I know not the reason.' Mo Ye said, 'I have heard it said that for the fusion of these heaven-sent metals, human sacrifice is needed. I'm afraid you cannot make the sword without human sacrifice.' Gan Jiang replied, 'I think of the past when my master was about to prepare the liquid for the making of a sword, the husband and wife both leapt into the furnace, only then did the metals fuse. Now men who seek the metals in the mines would wear mourning clothes, only then would they dare to get the metals. If I cannot make the metals fuse, it must be for this reason.' Mo Ye responded, 'If you know that, what is the difficulty?'

At this Gan Jiang's wife cut off her hair and threw it, with her nail clippings, into the furnace. She asked three hundred girls and boys to use the bellows and put charcoal into the furnace. The metals fused and the sword could be made. The male sword was called Gan Jiang and the female Mo Ye. The male sword was decorated with square characters like the tortoise, and the female sword was

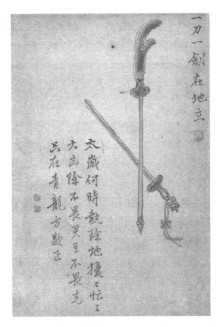

An illustration of swords from a nineteenth-century edition
of the Tang-dynasty *Tui Bei Quan Tu*, a collection of prophecies.

decorated with flowing characters. Gan Jiang hid the male
sword, but gave the female to King He Lu, who greatly
prized it.

It does not stretch the imagination too much, or indeed the language, to have Mo Ye throw herself into the furnace to appease the
gods of metallurgy. Many folktales tell of the human sacrifice that
is required for anything to do with the foundry. One legend from
Beijing told how the bell that tolled mournfully from its belltower
was the cry of the woman who sacrificed herself for its creation by
leaping into the caster's furnace.

But if Mo Ye did perform this ultimate self-sacrifice as recounted above, we would not have the second part of the story, which is a revenge drama. This version of the story is told in the *Soushen Ji* ('In Search of the Supernatural'), which was written in the Jin period (266–420 CE), some time after the collapse of the Han dynasty. In this story, the action has moved from Wu to Chu. Mo Ye is pregnant with their child, who grows up to avenge his father, whom the king killed in anger:

> In Chu, Gan Jiang and Mo Ye were making two swords, male and female, for the king. Three years had passed and they had not produced anything. The king was angry and wished to execute them. At the time the wife was heavily pregnant. The husband said to the wife, 'I have been making swords for the king for three years without success. The king is angry with me. If I go to him, he will surely put me to death. If you give birth to a male child, when he grows to adulthood, tell him: "If on coming out of the house he looks to the southern hills, where a pine tree grows from a stone, he will find the sword, hidden at its back."' He then took the female sword and went to see the King of Chu. The king was greatly angered and said to him, face to face, 'This sword has a male and a female: you have brought the female, but not the male.' The king had him executed.
>
> The son of Mo Ye was named Chi Bi. He grew up big and strong. One day he asked his mother, 'Where is my father?' His mother said, 'Your father was making swords for the King of Chu. It took him three years. The king

was angry and had him executed. When he went away he instructed me: "Tell your son: if he goes out of the house and looks towards the southern hills, where a pine grows out of a stone, the sword is hidden at its back."' Chi Bi then went out of the house and looked towards the south, there was no hill. But he saw before the house a pine pillar on a base of stone. He opened up the back of the pillar with an axe and got hold of the sword. All day and night, he thought of how he could take vengeance on the King of Chu.

The king had a dream: a man with a foot wide between his eyebrows was determined to take vengeance and kill him. The king put a thousand pieces of gold on the young man's head. When the son heard of this, he ran away, and he went into the hills, singing and weeping at the same time. A stranger met him and asked, 'You are but young, why are you crying so bitterly?' He replied, 'I am the son of Gan Jiang and Mo Ye. The King of Chu has killed my father, I want to avenge him.' The stranger said, 'I have heard that the king put a thousand pieces of gold on your head. Give me your head and the sword, and I will exact your vengeance for you.' The child then said, 'That would be excellent!' He immediately killed himself by cutting off his own head, and with both hands presented it and the sword to the stranger, but his corpse stood upright. The stranger said, 'I will not fail you.' The corpse then fell down.

The stranger, holding the head, went to see the King of Chu, who was greatly pleased. The stranger said, 'This is the head of a brave man, and it must be boiled in a large cauldron [to avoid it becoming a fiend].' The king did that, but despite boiling for three days and nights the head did not dissolve, and it jumped out of the cauldron with angry looks. The stranger now said, 'The child's head will not dissolve. Let the king come and look on it, it will surely dissolve.' The king went up close to it, and the stranger cut off his head with the sword he had been given, and the king's head dropped into the hot water. The stranger then cut off his own head, which also fell into the vat of hot water. The three heads all dissolved and could not be distinguished. People separated the flesh from the boiling water and buried it all, and they called the burial place the Tomb of the Three Kings. Now it is to the north of Runan in the county of Yichun.

This is one of the most famous of the tales in the *Soushen Ji*. We know nothing about the *ke*, which I have translated as 'stranger', but could also mean a 'guest' or 'wanderer'. Yet in this context it could also be read as *xiake*, 'a chivalrous guest/wanderer', or *jianke*, 'a wanderer with a sword', both of which we might recognize as a 'chivalrous knight', or what the Japanese might term *ronin*, a 'lowly person with a code of conduct behind him', which made the son of Mo Ye trust him.

SACRED RIVERS AND MOUNTAINS

Severe climatic events appear frequently in the mythologies of agricultural societies, whose survival depended on the reliable bounty of the land. Drought, personified in Ba (see p. 89), could bring crop failure and famine. Yi the Archer shot down nine of the original ten scorching suns and thus staved off calamity (p. 54). Floods, too, occur frequently in Chinese stories, appearing in texts from Zhou times onwards. This is hardly surprising: the great Yellow River that fertilized the plains of northern China dictated the fortunes of the people living on its banks, infusing the land with life-giving nutrients but also capable of destroying crops and settlements, especially after the spring melt in the Himalayas. No wonder, then, that saviour gods powerful enough to stem the flood, like Gun and Yu, were extremely popular, and their stories repeated over centuries. From the very earliest times the Chinese sought to propitiate the demons they believed controlled these dangerous natural forces. Sacred watercourses and peaks appear

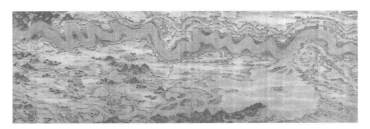

Detail from a Qing-dynasty scroll painting, *Ten Thousand Miles along the Yellow River.*

throughout Chinese mythology, and under the Zhou it was the emperor who was responsible for the ritual sacrifices that kept the mountain and great river spirits appeased.

DRAGONS

Few images are associated more strongly with China than the dragon, which was a very different creature from its western cousins. While in the west the dragon was a symbol of evil, usually depicted surrounded by human bones and treasure in deep, dank caves, or in combat with a human hero, the Chinese dragon was an intensely noble and largely benign spirit that dwelt in the sky. It symbolized water, which nourished the land and allowed Chinese civilization to flourish, though it might in anger release great quantities of water, causing fearsome floods.

Yinglong: The Responding Dragon

One of the earliest mentions of this dragon comes when Yu tames the Yellow River; he is shown the way by Yinglong, the 'Responding Dragon'. One of the cryptic questions in the *Tian Wen* ('Heavenly Questions') asks, 'What did the winged dragon trace on the ground?', referring to Yinglong creating the paths of the Nine Rivers with its tail.

The Responding Dragon returns, in the *Shan Hai Jing* ('Classic of Mountains and Seas'), to aid Huang Di in fighting the war god Chiyou. Huang Di ordered the Responding Dragon to store up all the water and then use it to flood their opponent Chiyou; but their plan failed, and Chiyou was only defeated after the Goddess of Drought, Ba, came to their aid (see p. 88).

Qing-dynasty hanging scroll of the emperor Qianlong wearing dragon robes.

We find recognizable dragon motifs from Neolithic times onwards in China, on objects such as jade amulets and bronze vessels. The dragon was possibly the totem of the Xia dynasty, a kingdom that ruled *c*. 2070–1600 BCE. Recent excavations at Erlitou – presumed to be the Xia capital, complete with a royal palace and workshops – have unearthed from an elite burial an exquisite model of a dragon made from more than 2,000 pieces of turquoise. Gradually, the symbol of the dragon was restricted to imperial representations only, with its five claws that signified the emperor himself. By the Ming dynasty (1368–1644), the dragon was used in palaces as the insignia for his imperial majesty, and no commoner could use the sign of the dragon.

Sima Qian, in the *Shiji*, described how during the Xia period it was possible to tame dragons as we might train horses or dogs, possibly basing this material on earlier sources that are no longer extant: 'Heaven sent down two dragons, a male and a female. [Emperor] Kong Jia was not able to care for them, and he had lost the support of the Huanlong ["Dragon Raising"] Clan…. But one Liu Lei learned the technique of taming dragons from the Huanlong Clan and thus obtained service with Kong Jia. Kong Jia bestowed on him the name of Dragon Tamer.' Sadly, the story does not end well, for the dragon or its tamer: 'The female dragon died and Liu Lei fed it to the [emperor] of Xia. The emperor sent someone to demand more, and fearing that he would be punished, Liu Lei went elsewhere.'

Some of the earliest representations of the classical-era gods had dragon (or serpent) tails, as we see in depictions of Fuxi and Nuwa with dragon tails and human upper bodies carved into stones or painted on silk. There were different kinds of dragons, some with scales and some with nine horns (nine was a mystic number, although it was sometimes used simply to mean 'many'). Numerous gods would ride on dragons, in the way that people rode horses.

Because of its association with water, the dragon was appealed to in times of drought. Rain-making ceremonies often invoked dragons, who brought rain clouds when they appeared in the sky. *Duanwu*, the Dragon Boat Festival, which is celebrated on the fifth day of the fifth lunar month – thought to be an unlucky month – is one such ceremony. In south China, this is when the monsoon rains ought to arrive; if they did not, the harvest that year might fail. One explanation for the Dragon Boat Festival is that the racing of boats with painted dragons on their prows was supposed to stimulate the dragons to appear in the sky and bring rain.

A twentieth-century woodblock print depicting the Dragon Boat Festival.
The seal prints above contain wishes for the New Year.

Another explanation links the festival – and its tradition of throwing *zongzi* (sweet rice dumplings wrapped in bamboo leaves) into the water – to the poet and author of the *Tian Wen* ('Heavenly Questions'), Qu Yuan (*c.* 340–278 BCE). Qu Yuan, also revered as an upright official, once had a dream in which he complained that he was unable to eat any *zongzi* because evil dragons were eating them all. Therefore, people race dragon boats to scare away the evil dragons. An alternative version is that Qu Yuan, distressed at the state of the nation, committed suicide by throwing himself into the Miluo River. Local people who admired him greatly rowed out in dragon boats to try and find his body. They threw *zongzi* into the water to stop the fish eating his body, for it is very important in Chinese belief that a body be buried whole. This is another example of myths growing around a real historical figure: a folk festival with a magical element created in commemoration of a poet. The festival is widely celebrated today: everyone eats *zongzi*, although the dragon boat races take place mostly on southern China's rivers and lakes and not in the dry north.

People would also appeal to dragons for good fortune for the coming year, especially during the Lantern Festival, which takes place on the fifteenth day of the first month of the lunar calendar. On this day, lanterns painted to resemble parts of a dragon are assembled together and paraded throughout the streets, so that it seems as if one long dragon is visiting the town. Sometimes a separate lantern marks the pearl, a symbol of wisdom, which the lantern-dragon chases after as dragons were believed to do. Though these dragon

A Qing-dynasty porcelain snuff bottle
decorated with a dragon chasing a pearl.

performances were once forbidden in China, they have been revived in China itself and in Chinatowns all over the world. In the power and auspiciousness of the dragon, we see the influence of Buddhism, where the *naga* of Indian descent have mixed with the Chinese legend of the dragon. The Indian Buddhist *naga* were half-human, half-cobra, frightening and powerful beings that could nevertheless come to the aid of people in distress.

HEBO: GOD OF THE YELLOW RIVER

Of all the deities associated with specific waterways – and there were many – the God of the Yellow River (Huang He) was by far the most important. The river, which passes through most of the North China Plain, takes its name from the sand that it picks up in the Loess Plateau, turning its waters a muddy yellow. As the river is very long, different regions along it developed their own stories of the God of the Yellow River. One of his names was Hebo. He was an unpredictable and sometimes vicious god, much like the river itself, which is sometimes referred to as 'China's Sorrow' because of the catastrophe it wrought before modern engineering mitigated the effects of its flooding.

There is a brief mention of Hebo in Qu Yuan's *Tian Wen*, which alludes to a story in which Hebo is shot by Yi the Archer (see p. 54), who abducted Hebo's wife Mifei, the goddess of the River Luo. Wang Yi (89–158 CE), who compiled and annotated the *Chu Ci* ('Songs of Chu'), made the following comment on an account attributed to Qu Yuan: 'Hebo changed into a white dragon and swam near the water. Yi saw him, shot him, and wounded him in the left eye. Hebo went

Hebo, the God of the Yellow River. From a fourteenth-century
album of eleven paintings relating to the *Nine Songs*.

to complain to the Supreme God, "Kill Yi for me". The Supreme God
asked him, "Why were you shot?" Hebo said, "At that time I changed
into a white dragon and went out." The Supreme God replied, "If you
had carefully guarded your godliness, how could Yi touch you? If
you were a reptile, of course you would be shot at by a man, which
would be right. What wrong has Yi done?'"

Because of the grave threat of flood that the Yellow River presented, many elaborate propitiation rites were developed along
its banks. One of these was brought to an abrupt end by Ximen
Bao, a hydraulic engineer and court advisor to Marquess Wen of
Wei (r. 445–396 BCE), during the Warring States period. In the *Shiji*,

Hebo rides in a chariot pulled by the dragons
of the Yellow River.

Sima Qian tells us that Ximen Bao was an early rationalist who abolished the annual practice of offering a human sacrifice to Hebo in Ye County, Henan Province. Previously a virgin girl had been chosen for her prettiness, dressed like a bride, and placed on a mattress that was floated downstream until it sank. Ximen Bao ostensibly objected to the girl not being pretty enough – in truth, he had discovered that the sacrifice was a stunt, enforced by corrupt officials to intimidate locals into paying high taxes – and heaved into the river a shaman to find out if Hebo was satisfied with her or not. When this shaman did not return, he pitched in another. When this one did not return from their consultation either, he suggested throwing in all the officials of the area, 'to find out'. They were all so terrified that the people of Ye ceased the custom. Ximen Bao then directed a programme of canal-building in the region, so that the river seldom flooded and local agriculture flourished.

GODDESSES OF THE XIANG RIVER

Perhaps the most famous water deities in China were the two daughters of the legendary emperor Yao: Ehuang and Nuying. They had married Yao's successor, Shun, and upon Shun's death they went to mourn him at his grave on the Xiang River, weeping so much that they stained the bamboos that grew along its banks (see p. 112). The

Fourteenth-century ink drawings of Ehuang and Nuying, the goddesses of the Xiang River. From an album of eleven paintings relating to the *Nine Songs*.

boat that they took met with bad weather, and they drowned in the river. Their spirits dwell in the Dongting Lake in Hunan Province. In the *Shan Hai Jing* ('Classic of Mountains and Seas'), we read how they 'often wander over the deep waters of the river.... And every time they wander in or out there is bound to be mighty winds and driving rain. There are many strange gods there....There are many strange birds.' When Qin Shi Huangdi, the First Emperor of China, visited the temple of Xiang Mountain he encountered a terrible storm, and learned that this was the place where the daughters of Yao were buried. They continued to be worshipped into the Tang period.

MOUNT KUNLUN

The mythical Mount Kunlun, abode of the gods, was a paradise that lay somewhere in the west (or possibly south – our sources are contradictory) of China's vast landscape. Whether it can be linked to the mountain range known as the Kunlun today, which lies north of the Tarim Basin in western China, is hard to say. Although this chain of mountains sits beyond the area controlled by the Chinese in the ancient era, the imposing snowy summits would have been visible from quite a distance all year round. Moreover, the Han Emperor Wu (r. 141–87 BCE) dispatched the explorer Zhang Qian in 139 BCE to seek allies in the region to counter the threat posed by the nomadic Xiongnu, a tribal group based in the Tarim Basin. His extraordinary journeys greatly enhanced the Han's knowledge of the region to the west and north of their frontiers, leading eventually to the establishment of the Silk Roads and China's dramatic expansion westward.

Song-dynasty ink drawing of the palaces of the gods on Mount Kunlun.

The otherworldly Mount Kunlun was believed to form an axis mundi, an epicentre of the universe where heaven and earth met. This earthly paradise was presided over by the Queen Mother of the West, Xiwang Mu, who lived on the neighbouring Jade Mountain. Her characteristics and importance changed over time. We find the first mention of her on oracle bones from the Shang dynasty (see p. 33): 'If we make offerings to the Mother of the East and Mother of the West, there will be approval.' In the *Shan Hai Jing*, she is described in one passage thought to record a third-century BCE text: 'There is a place called Jade Mountain, which is where the Queen Mother of the West lives. Her appearance is as a person, but she has the tail of a leopard, the teeth of a tiger, and she is good at making a noise which people call *xiao*. On her unkempt hair she wears a *sheng* headdress [or crown]. She controls the pestilences from heaven and the five punishments.' In a later chapter, possibly from the second century BCE, she wears the *sheng* headdress and holds a staff (or sceptre) while reclining on a bench; to the south there were 'three blue birds for her', which had 'red heads with black eyes'. In these texts the Queen Mother of the West not only presided over Mount Kunlun's earthly paradise, but sent plagues and punishments down on humanity. She also gave the elixir of immortality to Yi the Archer, which his wife, Chang'e, then stole for herself (see p. 57).

As time passed and the values of Chinese society changed, Xiwang Mu was transformed from an avenging deity into a more benign goddess. In the *Mu Tianzi Zhuan* ('Tale of Emperor Mu') – probably a post-Han fictional romance produced in the fourth or fifth centuries CE, despite being found allegedly among the third-century BCE

Xiwang Mu, the Queen Mother of the West, rides on a phoenix, accompanied by her retinue.

The Bamboo Annals

In 281 CE the *Zhushu Jinian* ('Bamboo Annals'), a chronicle of ancient China, were discovered in the tomb of King Xiang (d. 296 BCE) of Wei, one of the seven major states during the Warring States period. The Annals were written on bamboo strips using an ancient calligraphic script that was subsequently abolished, in 213 BCE, by Qin Shi Huangdi, First Emperor of China, when he introduced a uniform writing system that lasted more or less until the twentieth century. The original Annals have been lost, and our sources come from extracts in the works of pre-Song dynasty writers.

Zhushu Jinian ('Bamboo Annals') – the Queen Mother of the West exchanged diplomatic gifts and verses with Emperor Mu, who was recorded as the fifth ruler of the Zhou dynasty. By the time the 'Tale of Emperor Mu' was written, Xiwang Mu was partnered with Dongwang Gong ('King Father of the East'), about whom we know little, and had become an important deity to be worshipped as Daoism grew in influence. Even as late as the Ming dynasty (1368–1644) she was known affectionately but respectfully as Wang Mu Niangniang ('Queen Wang Mu').

The mystic number eight (for harmony, a number associated with all things lucky) and nine (for the nine heavens, another lucky number associated with the emperor) and detailed, gigantic measurements appear in the following description from the *Shan Hai Jing* ('Classic of Mountains and Seas'):

> Mount Kunlun is the area within the seas, in the northwest, that was the earthly dwelling place of the Heavenly God. Mount Kunlun occupies an area of eight hundred

li [300 miles] square, its height is that of eight thousand *zhang* [96,000 feet]. On its summit is a tree that grows [magic] grain, which is four *zhang* [48 feet] high, and five men could hug its girth. On the mountain there are nine wells on each side, and every well is surrounded by jade balustrades. There are nine gates, each one is guarded by a supernatural animal called Kaiming. This is where the myriad gods live. These gods live in the eight-sided cliff, by the bank of the Chishui ('red water') River. Unless you are a hero like Yi the Archer who shot the suns, do not think you can climb this cliff.

The ferocious Kaiming, a beast with the body of a tiger and nine human heads, guarded Jade Mountain along with an array of other fierce creatures, including serpents, felines, birds of prey and birds of paradise, and a dragon. As well as twelve jade trees (jade being associated with the divine) there was a giant tree, the Tree of Grain, that formed a ladder between earth and heaven. Such 'skyladders' are frequently mentioned in mythic texts such as the *Huainanzi* and the *Shan Hai Jing*. The god Taihao (see p. 77) was also associated with the giant *jianmu*, or 'the building tree': 'The *Jian* tree on Mount Duguang, by which the gods ascend and descend [to and from heaven], casts no shadow at midday....it forms a canopy over the centre of the world.' There are many versions of the *jianmu*. Even magical mountains such as the Kunlun itself could be skyladders, where shamans could reach heaven from earth.

It was on Mount Kunlun that Nuwa and Fuxi, the only people to survive the flood, married and had children (see p. 69). Many later legends tell of this place; it remained an important one throughout

Chinese mythology and legends. This magical mountain, said to exist in the deep south or west, should be distinguished from the real Kunlun range that lies north of the Tarim Basin in China's far northeast and only gained its name in the Han dynasty as Chinese explorers travelled along the Silk Road.

THE ISLES OF THE BLESSED: PENGLAI, FANZHANG AND YINGXIA

Far from Mount Kunlun in the west, three more mythical mountains lay in the Eastern Sea. These were islands where immortals dwelt with fabulous beasts in palaces made of precious metals. According to a Tang-dynasty commentator on Sima Qian's *Shiji*, 'All flora and fauna were white in colour, and the palaces and gates were made of gold and silver'. The isles appeared and disappeared at the whim of the immortals: 'They were like clouds as one gazed upon them from afar, but when one did get there the three spirit islands turned upside down beneath the water.' Mirages that occur on the east coast, as can often be seen from Qingdao on the Shandong Peninsula, may explain these strange appearances and disappearances.

The First Emperor, Qin Shi Huangdi (see p. 84), sought eternal life, consulting soothsayers and shamans in his quest. In 216 BCE he sent a band of boys and girls to contact the immortals on the fabled isles in the Eastern Sea, but they did not return. It was said by some that they founded the island of Japan. Four years later, a subsequent expedition failed to reach the islands, after being frightened off by an enormous fish. Later, the emperor himself went in search of this fish, armed with a crossbow, but failed to find it and died soon after.

THE FIVE GREAT MOUNTAINS

As well as mythical mountains, there were five real peaks that were sacred from the early days of the Zhou period, which straddled the known world of China in classical times and were revered as places where gods and humans could meet. These Five Great Mountains, the *Wuyue*, stood in the Five Directions significant in Chinese belief. They were: Huashan in the west (Shaanxi Province); Hengshan in the south (Hunan Province); Hengshan (written with different characters) in the north (Hebei Province); Songshan in the centre (Henan Province); and, most important of all, Taishan in the east (Shandong Province). None of these mountains is much higher than 1,500 metres (4,920 feet), but they would nonetheless have stood out from the mainly flat plain along the Yellow River in north China, where Chinese civilization started.

A Qing-dynasty handscroll illustration of the southern sacred peak of the Hengshan mountains.

A handscroll depicting Emperor Kangxi's inspection tour of the south.
This scroll shows his journey from Ji'nan to Mount Tai, 1698.

Lying in the east, where the divinity of spring resided, Taishan
(Mount Tai), was worshipped as the source of life for the whole of
China. In 219 BCE the First Emperor held a sacrificial ceremony on
its summit and set up an inscription declaring the greatness of his
rule. Subsequent emperors made pilgrimages to Taishan and the other
Five Great Mountains, effectively marking the bounds of their empire,
right up to the end of imperial rule in 1911. Taishan today preserves
aspects of imperial patronage such as the tomb of the white mule,
which died after carrying Emperor Taizong (of the Tang dynasty) up
the mountain. He granted it the title of 'general' and had it buried
with pomp. There is the weathered 'stele with no words' said to have
been erected by the First Emperor near the pine tree, under which he
sheltered from a thunderstorm and which he ennobled as an official
of the fifth rank. There are also Buddhist and Daoist temples and
shrines to local deities such as Bixia Yuanjun, the Princess of the
Azure Clouds, also known as the Holy Mother of Mount Tai. She is
an example of a possibly real person who was raised to the status of
goddess in the Song dynasty, said to be a princess who refused to

marry and instead went off to the mountain of Taishan and became a celestial immortal. She was regarded as a protector, rather like the Buddhist goddess Guanyin, and associated with childbirth. There were 102 temples to her in Qing-dynasty Beijing.

Mountains allowed the closest communication with the gods and were seen as the abode of benevolent, potentially rain-bearing dragons, swirling in the clouds. Buddhism adopted four sacred mountains of its own, each devoted to the worship of a major Bodhisattva: Wutaishan associated with Manjusri; Emeishan, the abode of Samantabhadra; Putuoshan, the seaside abode of Guanyin (Avalokitesvara); and Jihuashan, where the Bodhisattva Ksitigarbha, who presides over the underworld, is worshipped by devout people coming from all over China after a bereavement, asking for Ksitigarbha's intervention to see the soul of the dead escorted safely to paradise.

The Daoists, too, had four holy mountains: Qingchengshan, Wudangshan, Longhushan and Qiyunshan. Qingchengshan, near Chengdu in Sichuan, was revived early after the end of the Cultural Revolution and has a community of Daoist priests and many visitors.

7

BUDDHIST INFLUENCES

The legends of the post-classical era, after the fall of the Han dynasty, are much more detailed than earlier stories handed down through the oral tradition. They reflect society in the age of empire, for instance, the civil service examination system and bureaucracy. They also feature a far more diverse array of gods that show clearly in their traits and interactions the influence of a new cult from the west: Buddhism.

A page from a Ming-dynasty *Diamond Sutra* illustrating temples and deities of Mahayana Buddhism.

BUDDHISM

The arrival of Buddhism from India in the first century CE heralded a major change in Chinese history. It was the first time that aspects of a civilization comparable to China in wealth and power had penetrated the culture. Previously, the Chinese empire had borrowed ideas and technologies from the ethnic groups on its fringes that it considered 'inferior' to itself, but had encountered nothing as complex or alien as Indian civilization. What Buddhism offered was a totally different view of religion and of life; scholars say that its effect was ultimately not dissimilar to that of the western impact on China during the latter half of the nineteenth and beginning of the twentieth centuries.

When Buddhism first arrived in China during the Han dynasty, it was in some ways taken up as a branch of Daoism. Daoist terminology was used to translate Sanskrit terms, and Daoism had a similar interest in the practice of ascetic meditation. But very soon, by the time the first manuscripts were written in the Dunhuang area in the 4th century CE, it emerged as a new religion. Buddhism was a faith of personal salvation, a concept totally new to the Chinese. Buddhists believed that all human suffering derived from their existence on earth, and that the human soul migrated into another body at death, a process known as *samsara*, or metempsychosis. The result of this migration depended on how a person conducted themselves in their previous existence, or their 'karma' (from the Sanskrit *karman*, 'act'). A person could enter 'nirvana' – the ultimate state of peace, beyond craving and desire – only through good karma, releasing the individual from the cycle of suffering that each earthly existence entailed. According to Mahayana Buddhism, the school

The *Luohan*

Both Bodhisattvas and *luohan* (*arhat* in Sanskrit) were beings who, because of their holy deeds, achieved nirvana but decided to stay behind in order to help humanity. The four great Bodhisattvas, particularly emphasized in Mahayana Buddhism, which was the dominant influence on Chinese Buddhism, have a special place close to the Buddha and the assemblage of *luohan* are often depicted in separate rooms in a temple. Though there were only six *arhats* in Indian Buddhism, there are a variety of groupings in Chinese temples, from twelve to as many as 500.

In the Ming-dynasty scroll *The Sixteen Luohans*, the *luohan* is presented as an archaic and eccentric figure surrounded by nature.

of thought that became prevalent in China, upon reaching nirvana a person attains Buddhahood, the 'awakened' or enlightened state. There is also an in-between state of Bodhisattvahood, in which a person's imminent liberation is delayed so that they may work for the salvation of others.

The White Horse Temple in Luoyang, established under
the patronage of Emperor Ming in 68 CE.

We find the first evidence of Buddhism in China at Luoyang,
the Eastern Han capital in Henan Province, where the White Horse
Temple was established in 68 CE. The buildings today date mainly
from the Ming, with heavy restoration in recent decades. A traditional Chinese temple consisting of a series of courtyards and halls,
it includes two stone statues of horses, probably Song in date. Behind
the main hall, steps lead up to the Cool Terrace, said to have been
constructed for the two Indian Buddhist founders of the temple
to translate the sutras. It is very likely that Buddhism arrived with
traders from western Central Asia, via what would become the Silk
Roads. The earliest Chinese translations of Buddhist texts were
introduced by the Parthians, a major ancient Iranian empire roughly
contemporaneous with the Han dynasty. One such cultural mediator
was An Shigao, who settled in Luoyang around 148 CE and is said to
have produced some 200 translated works. These translations were

rather loose and imprecise, with an immigrant Buddhist explaining the source text to a native Chinese speaker, who in turn depended on a Chinese scribe to write down the text. Han Buddhism recruited its first true believers from Daoist circles, so there was a tendency towards Daoist interpretations.

Many Buddhist monks followed in the early missionaries' footsteps, but it was the translations of Kumarajiva (334–431) from the Buddhist Kingdom of Kucha that proved most acceptable to the elite Chinese, and thereafter translations of Buddhist texts slowly permeated the whole of East Asia. Chinese monks now journeyed to India, pilgrims such as Faxian (337–442), who travelled there to obtain the 'true scriptures (*sutras*) of Buddhism', and who only returned to Nanjing after having wandered through Southeast Asia on ships that were beaten by storms. The seventh-century CE Buddhist monk

A Tang-dynasty illustration of the Buddhist monk Xuanzang on his journey, carrying a backpack of scrolls, holding a staff and accompanied by a tiger.

Xuanzang's journey to India was fictionalized in the Ming-dynasty classic *Xi You Ji* ('Journey to the West') (see p. 169); though his actual adventures, which we can reconstruct from Tang-dynasty records, were equally exciting. He slipped out of China despite Emperor Taizong's proscription on foreign travel, and then travelled for seventeen years, seeking out and studying under many of the best-known scholars in India. In the last years of his life, which he spent in the Chinese capital Chang'an (today Xi'an), he translated a large number of Buddhist texts and was greatly admired, especially by his disciples, who wrote biographies chronicling his deeds.

As Buddhism became better known in China, the new gods from India became popular, often with a traditional Chinese twist.

GUANYIN

By far the most popular Buddhist deity in China is Guanyin, the goddess of mercy and compassion. Her name translates as 'the one who looks down on the world and hears its cries'. Her image can be found everywhere, including in many homes, and there are temples to her across the country. Originally she was an Indian Bodhisattva in Mahayana Buddhism by the name of Avalokitesvara, which in China could be male or female (representations before the twelfth century reveal a small moustache), though in India remained strictly male. Her cult quickly spread all over East Asia. Since compassion was linked more closely with womanhood in China, she very quickly became a goddess amongst the Chinese, who had never had such a major goddess before. To this day, she is worshipped among Chinese Buddhists as a saviour, especially from perils at sea and in childbirth.

A Ming-dynasty ink drawing of the Bodhisattva Guanyin
and the sixteen *luohans* on the island of Mount Putuo.

It is probable that earlier local goddesses, who were prayed to for similar protections, became amalgamated with her.

Guanyin's cult was centred around Mount Putuo, an island southeast of Shanghai in the Zhoushan archipelago, Zhejiang Province. She was first worshipped there some time in the seventh century CE, during the Tang dynasty. The story goes that a Japanese monk was trying to take her statue back to Japan with him, but a storm arose and he was obliged to take shelter on Mount Putuo. He decided that the statue did not want to leave China, so he left it on the island and built a nunnery called 'Reluctant to Leave Monastery', which through various incarnations still exists today.

Buddhist Goddess or Chinese Princess?

Some early Chinese scholars believed that Guanyin was an ancient Chinese princess by the name of Miaoshan. Miaoshan's father, a cruel king, attempted to force her to marry a man against her will; yet she had made a vow to become a Buddhist nun and resisted. She begged to be allowed to join a monastery, and eventually the king relented, but ordered the monks to give her the most unpleasant tasks. She happily did everything that was asked of her. Her father, enraged, ordered his forces to burn down the convent where she had taken refuge, but Miaoshan put out the flames, and so he commanded that she be put to death. Years later, the king was stricken with illness. He was told that the only cure was an eye and a hand from a person willing to sacrifice them for him. He could find no one to do that, except Miaoshan, who had gone to the Underworld. Nevertheless, she gave him one of her eyes and her hand; he was cured, and she was transformed into the goddess of mercy, Guanyin, who is sometimes depicted with a halo of a thousand eyes.

The Tale of Shancai

Shancai (also called Sudana in Sanskrit) often appears in Chinese folk stories as an acolyte of Guanyin. It was said that he was a disabled beggar boy in India who wanted to learn the Buddha's teachings, and so he journeyed to Mount Putuo, having heard that there was a Bodhisattva there willing to teach him. When he arrived, Guanyin decided to test him, conjuring illusions of monsters that chased after her. He ran as best as he could and threw himself off a cliff while chasing away the monsters, but Guanyin rescued him in mid-air. He then found that he could walk with ease again, and became her devoted servant.

Often, statues of Guanyin show her carrying a fish basket. This comes from a legend that involved the Dragon King, whose son, in the shape of a fish, was caught by a fisherman. The Dragon King could do nothing to save him, but Guanyin heard the prince's cries, and sent her servant to buy the fish at whatever cost. This caused a sensation in the market, but Guanyin was able to shame all the other people who tried to buy the fish, and her servant bought and released it into the sea. One version says that the Dragon King was so grateful that he gave Guanyin the 'Pearl of Light' that shone always. That is why statues of Guanyin are found with a basket of fish on her arm, and also sometimes with the Pearl of Light. The custom of releasing fish and other animals for the pot from captivity still exists, and partly comes from this legend.

A Qing-dynasty glazed porcelain figurine of Guanyin holding a fish basket.

MAZU

Another protector goddess of the seas is Mazu (meaning 'mother' or 'maternal ancestor'), also known as 'Queen of Heaven'. Originally a Daoist figure, she was worshipped along the shore of the South China Sea, where storms and typhoons are especially frequent, from Fujian to Taiwan and Hong Kong (where she is known as Tin Hau, Heavenly Empress). Festivals devoted to Mazu are still celebrated on the twenty-third day of the third month of the lunar calendar.

A statue of Mazu, from the Tianhou Temple, Tianjin.

Mazu's origins are uncertain. In some traditions she is said to be based on a woman named Lin Mo; exactly when she lived is uncertain, but her cult was established by the thirteenth century. One source tells us that she was a shaman from Fujian Province who lived in the tenth century. She is often confused with Guanyin, so much so that Guanyin was supposed to have been incarnated as Mazu. In another legend, Mazu became so entranced by Guanyin that she became a Buddhist.

RULAI FO: THE CHINESE BUDDHA

Siddhartha Gautama or Sakyamuni ('the sage from the tribe of the Sakyas') Buddha, best known simply as the Buddha, was the historic founder of Buddhism. Buddhist temples – including those in China – preserve in their main hall effigies to Gautama, the highest god of Buddhism. He came to China under various titles, and is most often named Rulai Fo.

Buddhist temples were everywhere in China, in specific sites such as the Buddhist holy mountains, but there were many in every town and city as Buddhism was the most widely practised popular religion in China. In eighteenth- and nineteenth-century Beijing there were hundreds of Buddhist temples and shrines in the city and its environs. Buddhist temples were constructed as a series of courtyards and halls with the living quarters of the monks at the rear. Inside the main gate there were great stucco statues of the four Heavenly Kings in full armour, often depicted trampling on evil spirits. They are Indian Buddhist *lokapalas*, protectors of Buddhism and thus also of the temple. In their Chinese embodiment

A colossal statue of Buddha, including an altar and offerings, at the Kwang Hau Temple in Guangzhou.

they are: the black-faced Guardian of the North, who holds a pearl and a snake; the red-faced Guardian of the South, who carries an umbrella with which he can conjure up thunderstorms; the blue-faced Guardian of the East, who carries a musical instrument and can summon an army of musicians; and the white-faced Guardian of the West, who wields a sword and leads an army of serpent-gods. In the next courtyard, facing the main Buddhist statues in the main hall, there is often a depiction of Budai (see p. 159) the fat, 'laughing' Buddha. The main hall in any temple displays a statue of the Buddha, sometimes accompanied by Bodhisattvas or other figures, such as the Buddha of Medicine, and behind this main set of statues there is often a depiction of Guanyin.

AMITABHA: THE PRINCIPAL MAHAYANA BUDDHA

Amitabha ('Infinite Light') is the principal Buddha in the Pure Land sect of Mahayana Buddhism, which was invented in China and is also known as Chan Buddhism ('Zen' in Japanese). Amitabha rules over the Pure Land of the West, a celestial realm, together with Rulai Fo and the Bodhisattva Guanyin. Mahayana Buddhism teaches that one can attain rebirth in the Pure Land through meditative practice by chanting 'Amituofo', a combination of Amitabha's name and *tuofo*, meaning 'for the sake of the Buddha'.

A Qing-dynasty embroidery of the Amitabha Buddha.

BUDAI: THE LAUGHING BUDDHA

You often see the figure of the Laughing Buddha, a fat, smiling man with an exposed stomach, depicted in Chinese art and iconography, and he is found in many temples. He is a Chan (Pure Land) Buddhist character, a poor but contented monk said to have lived in the tenth century CE, who wrapped his few possessions in a bundle of cloth that he carried around with him on a staff. The *budai*, or 'cloth sack', became his insignia as well as his name. In true Indian Buddhist fashion, he begged for his food, wandering amid the population and laying down to sleep anywhere, regardless of the weather. He was loved for his charismatic, easygoing and content nature, and is often depicted surrounded by children. He is also said to be able to predict the future. Before he died, in 917 according to one source, he claimed to be an incarnation of Maitreya, the Buddha of the Future: the successor to the Buddha Gautama, who will one day arrive on earth.

A Qing-dynasty porcelain Budai, with his laughing face and large, round stomach.

THE GODS OF THE UNDERWORLD

In ancient China people had only the vaguest concept of an Underworld; Confucius never pronounced on an afterlife and Daoism offered little solace to the bereaved. In Buddhism, however, the Bodhisattva Ksitigarbha (Di Zang) was said to rule over the Underworld, judging the sins of the dead, and the Bodhisattva Amitabha offered eventual salvation in a heavenly realm. And so Buddhism gave to the Chinese the concepts of an otherworldly realm where those who had done bad deeds in their lives met with punishments and the hope of paradise.

The Buddhist god Yama, known as Yanluo in China, passed judgment on the dead in the Underworld, which came to be known as Diyu. Diyu was imagined as a kind of labyrinth, with ten layers. Yanluo originally dwelt in the first layer, but because he was sympathetic to those who had died unjustly and released them to the world for reincarnation, he was banished to the fifth layer of hell, where the greatest of religious sinners are committed – those who killed living things. Yanluo did not have his own temple in China, for people believed it was unlucky to worship him. Instead, he was usually given space in the temple to the local god. Popular belief in China transformed the original Buddhist concept of the Underworld into a series of courts, in parallel with the bureaucratic legal system faced by the living, where judges presided over different courts to administer justice to those who had committed specific sins against the faith. It was believed that souls took 49 days to progress through this Buddhist legal system. After that, the relatives of the bereaved would make their way to a temple, making offerings to Amitabha, and chant his name to obtain release to paradise for the soul of the

五殿閻羅王

如壽夢有
輪流富貴
善興英雄料
免興帝三子

北柔香咋

Yanluo passes judgment on the dead
in the fifth layer of hell.

dead. Such ceremonies were revived after the Cultural Revolution and today many people make their way to Jiuhuashan, the mountain where Ksitigarbha, the Bodhisattva who presides over hell, a higher being than Yanluo, is particularly revered. There they pay for expensive and extensive masses for the dead, for feasts and the distribution of sweets to all present, and lead the chanting.

THE DUNHUANG CACHE

The popular influence and spread of Buddhism remained largely unknown until the early twentieth century, when a chance discovery revealed hidden records at Dunhuang, once a hub of the Silk Roads in China's northwestern Gansu Province. Here, in 1900, a Daoist priest named Wang Yuanlu found a remarkable cache of manuscripts in a walled-up part of the 'Caves of the Thousand Buddhas'. These proved to be documents of great antiquity, including the fragments of between 30,000 and 40,000 manuscripts dating from the fifth to the tenth centuries, largely devoted to Buddhism, mostly in Chinese, but with at least sixteen other languages represented. The cache was sealed up around 1000 CE, during the Song dynasty, possibly because these documents were considered to be 'sacred waste' at risk of destruction by marauders, such as the Tanguts of the once-powerful state of Xixia. The Dunhuang cache was a veritable gold mine for scholars: the manuscripts or their fragments contained the scribblings of sutras, of contracts and legal documents, of childish scribbles in schools, of popular songs and stories in a mixture of prose and verse – in fact, everything with writing on it had been treasured and hidden away. Their value was not only academic; Wang used the proceeds from selling the cache to restore his decrepit monastery.

Dunhuang lay near the Gobi and Taklamakan deserts, where the Silk Roads divided into northern and southern routes. The Silk Roads carried much more than silk, major religions travelled both ways: Buddhism, Nestorian Christianity and Islam. Traders brought all kinds of things, including animals – the Chinese were much intrigued by the ostrich – spices, wine and ceramics. These traders passed through the great Buddhist kingdoms of Kucha, Khotan

The Sale and Dispersal of the Dunhuang Cache

The Dunhuang cache came to light at a time when China had little global power and was vulnerable to foreign actors. Britain and Russia, mindful of possible incursions into their respective Indian and Central Asian territories, kept a watchful eye on each other, and Britain funded expeditions into Central Asia by the Hungarian explorer-cum-archaeologist Aurel Stein (1862–1943). During his second expedition he heard of the Dunhuang cache, and in 1907 persuaded the Daoist monk Wang to sell him some 7,000 complete manuscripts as well as thousands of other fragments. Stein knew no Chinese, so took what he could and brought his finds back to the British Museum. Upon further study, it transpired that many were copies of the same sutra. In later years, Chinese nationalists declared Stein a robber and staged protests against him. By then, however, many of the other Dunhuang documents had also been dispersed. In 1908, Paul Pelliot (1878–1945), a French sinologist who could read Chinese as well as several other languages, purchased 10,000 of the manuscripts from Wang and brought them to Paris. Subsequently other collectors heard of the cache, including Luo Zhenyu from Beijing. The Chinese were interested in mainly those documents in Chinese, ignoring most of those in other languages.

The result of this international competition for the cache is that today the manuscripts are scattered all over the world, appearing in collections in London, Paris, St Petersburg, Kyoto, Beijing and elsewhere. Fortunately, the International Dunhuang Project aims to conserve, catalogue and digitize them all, making them available for study worldwide.

and Loulan. The Chinese, however, sealed off access to their capital Chang'an (today Xi'an) during the wave of Buddhist persecutions at the end of the Tang dynasty and the turning inward of the Song dynasty. Traffic along the route decreased, a process accelerated by the disappearance of glaciers that irrigated the area and the arrival of Islamic warriors from the far west.

From the Dunhuang manuscripts we can gather that the arrival of Buddhist scriptures was closely connected to the beginning of vernacular literature in China. The cache is famous for containing the earliest appearance of the *bianwen*, a highly stylized form of literature blending prose and song that before the Dunhuang discovery had seemed to emerge much later in Chinese history. These tales tend to be very long, offering many descriptions of demons and the ways they inflict pain on men and women who have sinned, often accompanied by illustrations. Indeed, some scholars suspect that the antecedent of the *bianwen* was a type of picture storytelling transmitted to China from India. Some of the stories are narrated in a mixture of prose and verse. Entertainers, who would have had no knowledge of the classical works that gave rise to such legends, would have learnt the tales from their masters and applied the style of the *bianwen*.

BUDDHIST TALES FROM THE DUNHUANG CACHE

The *bianwen* found at Dunhuang are largely, though not all, related to Buddhism. The most popular of these tales are 'Mulian Rescues his Mother' and 'Wu Zixu', both of which are represented by more than one copy or fragment in Dunhuang's 'Caves of the Thousand Buddhas'. The former's origins are entirely in Buddhist India (the hero is given the name of Maudgalyayana, which the Chinese translators converted to 'Mulian'), while the latter concerns a folk hero from the time of China's Eastern Zhou dynasty (770–256 BCE).

The Legend of Mulian

This story refutes the idea that the tenets of Buddhism are fundamentally in opposition to Confucian notions of filial piety. In the Tang-dynasty versions found at Dunhuang, Mulian leaves his family to become a monk, and while away, both his parents die. He observes the traditional Confucian mourning period of three years, at the end of which he meets his father through Buddha. His father tells him that he and his wife acted differently in life, and so his mother has fallen into hell. Mulian is directed to the Avici Hell – the last and worst of all hells. When Mulian arrives at the seventh compartment, he finds his mother, the Lady Liu Qingti, undergoing horrendous punishments; she only recognizes him by his former

Mulian finds his mother suffering terrible punishments in hell.
From a nineteenth-century scroll painting.

nickname, Turnip. With the help of Buddha, she leaves the Avici Hell, but since all her previous sins of avarice have not been expiated she becomes a hungry ghost, whose food turns to fire in her throat. Buddha tells Mulian that he may only save her from this fate if he observes the 'Yulan bowl ritual', which is held on the fifteenth day of the seventh month in the lunar calendar, known as the Festival of Hungry Ghosts. Through Mulian's veneration of his mother, the Lady Liu Qingti was then incarnated as a black dog. Mulian found her and recited the Mahayana sutras for seven days. Then she was reincarnated as a human. This story is the origin of the Ghost Festival, celebrated in China to this day.

The Legend of Wu Zixu

This legend concerns a well-known folk hero from the Spring and Autumn period of the Zhou dynasty (*c.* 770–476 BCE). We meet this figure, Wu Zixu, in Sima Qian's *Shiji* ('Records of the Grand Historian'), written around 194 BCE, well before the advent of Buddhism. Yet in the Dunhuang *bianwen*, his tale is told with many references to Buddhist notions of good and evil, showing the influence of Buddhism on the evolution of Chinese legends.

The story is set in the kingdom of Chu. It begins with the king, Ping, putting Wu Zixu's father and elder brother to death upon suspicion of fomenting rebellion, and sending out a proclamation demanding Wu Zixu's head. Wu Zixu, hunted by the king's men, attempts to flee to the neighbouring kingdom of Yue. At the River Ying he meets a girl, who feeds him and, upon their parting, kills herself, so that he may rest in the knowledge that she will not betray him. Next, he meets his sister; her sons try to apprehend him, but he evades them. He arrives at his wife's house, where he begs for food and she recognizes him. After he leaves her, he knocks out his teeth, so that nobody else will recognize him. He then meets a fisherman, who persuades him to go to the kingdom of Wu rather than Yue; the fisherman, too, kills himself to set Wu Zixu's mind at ease. Wu Zixu becomes a great minister in the kingdom of Wu, and finally attacks and defeats the kingdom of Chu. Although King Ping is by now dead, Wu Zixu has him disinterred so his bones may be whipped, as retribution for the murder of his father and elder brother. Wu Zixu contrives to be a fine minister until the king of Wu dies, but he fails to get on with his successor, and is commanded to take his own life. Wu Zixu foresees the end of Wu and asks for his eyes to be suspended over the gates of the city so that he may see the conquering army of Yue. His prediction comes to pass; the story ends with the army of Yue coming to annihilate Wu.

In these stories, we see how Buddhism and Daoism combined to give rise to some of the most famous legends of China. We know little about how such tales developed, but several centuries later during the Ming dynasty (1368–1644), when printing had become highly developed, many were published, both in the form of novels and short stories. Thus, as we shall see in the next chapter, the *Journey to the West* tells the well-known tale of the Monkey King (or simply 'Monkey'), while the story of the 'Woman in White' gives us the legend of Madame White Snake.

8

LEGENDS OF THE MING DYNASTY

Before the discovery of the Dunhuang archive, our primary source for popular tales of the imperial era were Ming-dynasty (1368–1644) novels. These stories were already fully fledged, and presented by storytellers who performed at gatherings, such as at teahouses and festivals. These tales would also have been recounted in dramatic performances of which we have no trace, since the troupes of travelling actors rarely set down their words. Yet these performances clearly had a great impact on people's imaginations, and there are many characters from the Ming-dynasty novels who are celebrated in these plays.

During the Ming dynasty, there was a shift towards urbanization as towns grew larger, and a semi-literate class emerged including people such as merchants, who required a certain level of literacy to carry on their trade. These were not members of the small upper class whose children were trained to take the civil service examinations, and who knew the classics by heart. Rather, this was semi-literate gentry that learned to read Chinese characters and could appreciate the language in the form of written text. They formed an important new market for Ming publishers, who were at this time capable of mass-producing books, block-printing onto cheap paper. They started issuing a large number of novels, including historical romances; one of the most famous of these is *Xi You Ji* ('Journey to the West').

JOURNEY TO THE WEST

Journey to the West, which features the exploits of a travelling monk who is accompanied by the charming Sun Wukong (the 'Monkey King' or 'Monkey'), is one of the most popular Chinese novels, printed originally by several different publishers in the Ming dynasty. It was made famous in the west in an abridged version known as *Monkey: A Folk-tale of China* (1942), translated by Arthur Waley. Complete translations into English of all 100 chapters have since been published. A Japanese version for television, *Saiyuki*, was broadcast by the BBC in the 1980s (as *Monkey*), and China Central Television has likewise produced an adaptation. There were many antecedents to this marvellous book; suffice to say that the basic story was very popular from the thirteenth to the sixteenth centuries. We do not know for certain the name of the author, although it has been attributed to Wu Cheng'en (*c.* 1506–82), a writer who lived largely as a hermit in his native Jiangsu Province.

Journey to the West has been interpreted as the 'journey of man'. The main character, a monk named Tang Sanzang, sets out to collect the true sutras (scriptures) from their homeland, India. He is accompanied by his human flaws: his will or ambition, represented by Monkey, and his appetites, including greed and lechery, represented by Zhu Bajie ('Pigsy'). In fact, in the seventh century a monk called Xuanzang (602–664), who was given the title of Tripitaka ('Three Baskets' in the Buddhist canon) in honour of his Buddhist teachings, had indeed set out on such a quest. Xuanzang's real journey via the Silk Roads to India and Sri Lanka was chronicled by his disciples, and it contains fascinating stories. Yet these do not feature in the *Journey to the West*, the novel is a wholly fictional tale. The inspiration for Monkey is said to be the Indian monkey-god Hanuman, an important character in the great mythological epic the *Ramayana*.

There is a long introduction to the book proper (typical of popular fiction of the era), which tells of the exploits of Monkey. He was born from the piece of stone with which Nuwa, mother-goddess of humanity, mended heaven (see p. 66), and became leader of the other monkeys (who dub him the 'Monkey King') in the 'Paradise of Flowers and Fruit'. Upon his death, he was dragged to the Underworld, but instead of submitting to his fate he erased his name from the Book of the Dead, and so became immortal. He ascended into heaven, where he created havoc, angering several gods and coming to the attention of the Jade Emperor. Endeavouring to control him, the emperor gives him the lowly post of 'keeper of the heavenly horses'. Flying into a rage at this slight, Monkey is temporarily appeased by being appointed guardian of the heavenly peach garden, but soon rebels by eating almost all the peaches in the garden. All of this is recounted in the episode of the 'Great Havoc in Heaven', in which Monkey is imprisoned first by the legendary Daoist Laozi, then by the great Buddha, to await the coming of the monk from China who sets off for India. Only now does Tang Sanzang make his appearance in the novel, and from there the story focuses on his journey to the west.

Thanks to the much-loved goddess Guanyin (see p. 151), Tang Sanzang is able to recruit disciples, including Monkey and Pigsy. These pilgrims encounter fiends who are determined to devour Tang Sanzang, partly because by eating his flesh they might become immortal. Tang Sanzang is captured repeatedly by a whole host of demons and spirits, and it is left to his disciples to find a way to rescue him. Worst of all, however, is what they encounter at the very feet

Tang Sanzang, Pigsy and a disciple bow down to the goddess Guanyin while Monkey looks on. From a Qing-dynasty edition of *Journey to the West*.

of the Buddha, where they meet with the corruption that kills the best of intentions: the sutras that they obtain from the source of the religion are quite blank, because the pilgrims have failed to grease the palms of the creatures that loaded the sutras. When the Monkey rallies them all to protest about it to the Buddha himself, they are fobbed off with all sorts of excuses, such as that the people of China would not understand that the blank scriptures are more valuable. (How many times in history have people in China been fobbed off with the same kind of specious arguments?) Nevertheless, the story ends happily. Many demons are fought off by Monkey, who can pluck

Monkey battles the spider spirit. Qing-dynasty woodblock
illustration of a scene from *Journey to the West*.

hairs from his head that turn into fierce tigers or hundreds of little
monkeys. He fights monsters such as the Yellow Wing Monster or the
Daoist Master of the Yellow Flower Temple, who reduces Sanzang to
weakness by giving him poisoned tea. Monkey manages to subdue
him and his 'spider sisters', whereupon the Daoist Master reverts to
his real form of a seven-metre-long centipede and is killed by Pigsy.
The pilgrims also rescue 1,111 little boys who have been put in cages,
preventing them from being eaten by a king who wants to use them
to make an elixir of longevity. Having made up with those around
the Buddha through their relentless struggle against enemies of the
faith and been rewarded by the gift of hundreds of Buddhist sutras,

the pilgrims return to China, magically whirled through the air to their destination in Chang'an.

The book largely owes its popularity to the irreverent Monkey, who is full of mischief. Yet the story has also endured because of its subtle twists and turns, which show the characters clearly, such as the competition between Monkey and Pigsy, both of whom have skills that can be brought into the battles against demons but who are jealous of each other and only too happy to tell tales to Tang Sanzang. At one point he temporarily banishes Monkey because of the insinuations of Pigsy, only to have Pigsy plead for his return.

The structure of *Journey to the West* evidently originated in the performance of a storyteller, who regularly summarizes what has gone before so we can understand each episode very easily. In this way, we can see how the novel was based on individual plays or episodes that could be recounted in one night. Thanks to its psychological depth, the story has maintained its popularity over hundreds of years, and it is still regularly performed in China today in various media. Indeed, the rich characterization gave it a new lease of life as a favourite subject for new imaginings of the twentieth century, when western ideas about the novel as an artform entered China.

THE ROMANCE OF THE THREE KINGDOMS

The popular *San Guo Yan Yi* ('Romance of the Three Kingdoms'), another Ming-dynasty product, is familiar to all Chinese. It is a much romanticized historical novel that emerged out of the third-century CE historian Chen Shou's *Records of the Three Kingdoms*, a chronicle of the chaotic time after the decline of the Han empire in which the

Kingdoms of Wei, Shu and Wu competed for ultimate dominance over the course of the Three Kingdoms period (220–280 CE).

The story is full of action, following the various political machinations and military manoeuvres of the warlords who jockeyed for power. These were primarily Liu Bei, ruler of the Kingdom of Shu, and Cao Cao, head of the Kingdom of Wei, alongside a wider cast of characters from the upper classes of society. Liu Bei shared the surname of the dying Han-dynasty emperors, which made him the successor to the Han. Liu Bei formed an alliance with the generals Zhang Fei and Guan Yu in a famous scene pitched in the Peach Blossom Orchard.

The main theme of the novel is integrity, in all senses of the word. The collapse of the Han dynasty and the break-up of China

'Oath of the Peach Orchard.' Japanese painting on silk of a scene from *The Romance of the Three Kingdoms*.

Liu Bei, Zhang Fei and Guan Yu perform a sacrificial ceremony before taking the oath. From a Ming-dynasty edition of *The Romance of the Three Kingdoms.*

into separate warring states is viewed as a disaster. The novel begins with the phrase, 'The empire, long divided, must unite; long united, must divide', anticipating further periods of disunion at the fall of the Tang and the Song. The possibility of restoring central government depends upon the moral integrity of the main characters. The most intriguing is Zhuge Liang, a real historical figure, chief advisor to Liu Bei, whose cunning stratagems are the stuff of legend. Desperately short of arrows, he sent straw-packed boats past the enemy encampment on a riverbank and collected all the arrows they shot at these decoy boats, but his most famous achievement was the 'stratagem of

Guan Yu

The story goes that the general Guan Yu was captured by Cao Cao, who treated him very well. After Guan Yu was released, he never forgot the kindness Cao Cao showed him, and allowed the warlord to escape during times when the tables were turned, for Guan Yu, who was the epitome of loyalty and righteousness, could not bear to be indebted to anyone.

Guan Yu had the idealized male attributes of courage and good looks. He was brave in battle and could bear pain; in one famous incident, Guan Yu was dealt with an injury to his arm that left poison in the bone. While his arm was operated upon, he drank and played a game of chess. He was very tall and had an unusually full beard, which was considered especially handsome. His face was very red, and so whenever a red-faced man appears on stage in Chinese theatre, he is bound to be a 'good' man. In fact, whenever Lord Guan appeared he was always accompanied by drums and gongs. Lord Guan was adopted by members of cult societies for his loyalty and righteousness. He was also adopted by merchants as their patron who wished to emphasize that 'their word was their bond'.

the empty fortress'. Again, short of men and weapons, he occupied a walled fort and told his men to hide inside, leaving one or two sweeping the stones in the open gateway. Zhuge Liang sat above the gateway, playing his *guqin* (zither) peacefully. The enemy was lured into the apparently empty fortress and destroyed by the small but well-prepared force inside. Such stories of cunning and bravery have ensured that the novel remains popular to this day and, like *Journey to the West*, is retold in cartoons, television series and video games.

SHORT STORIES

Alongside the great novels penned in the Ming dynasty were many short stories that drew on, and in turn influenced, popular myths and legends. One of the foremost writers in this period was Feng Menglong (1574–1646), who edited and compiled ancient stories that he had heard, some of them in Classical Chinese, publishing a number of anthologies. Among the most famous of his stories is 'The Woman in White', in which we can see the triumph of Buddhism over Daoism (or China's folk religion). The use of the supernatural, a favourite theme in the old tales, is given a Buddhist twist. There have been many variations on this story, including modern operatic and cinematic retellings, and it is now considered one of China's most famous folktales.

The story appeared in Feng Menglong's *Xing Shi Heng Yan* ('Stories to Caution the World'), published in 1624, entitled 'The Woman in White captured forever under the Leifeng Pagoda'. It tells how the spirit, or *jing*, of a white water-snake was imprisoned under Leifeng Pagoda ('Thunder Peak'), a tower in Zhejiang Province, by a Buddhist monk called Fahai.

At the West Lake in the city of Hangzhou in Zhejiang Province lived a young man by the name of Xuxuan. Having been orphaned from an early age, he lived with his sister, and worked in a medicine shop owned by his brother-in-law and his family. Xuxuan returned by boat to the other side of the lake where he lived. Just as the boat was about to pull away, there came a shout from the shore, where a woman dressed in white wanted to cross the lake with her maid. The boat turned back and the two women got on. The Woman in White seemed to be in mourning and looked expensively clothed; her maid was dressed in blue. Once on board the Woman in White started a conversation with Xuxuan, telling him that she had recently lost her husband. They were getting on very well when the boat docked on the other shore. By then it had started to rain and Xuxuan had an umbrella, which he gallantly lent to the Woman in White. She was full of thanks and told him where she lived so he could reclaim his umbrella.

The next day he went to the Arrow Bridge in Hangzhou, where the Woman in White lived. He asked the neighbours in the area, but no one seemed to know of a recently widowed young lady. Fortunately, he caught sight of the maid out in the street, who led him to a large house nearby. The Woman in White received him in a beautifully decorated room and offered him food and drink. After a while, she spoke directly to him, saying that she had great affection for him,

Leifeng Pagoda

Leifeng Pagoda was not originally intended as a prison for the Woman in White. The eight-sided pagoda, one of the ten sights of the West Lake of Hangzhou, was built in 795 by the local king for his favourite concubine. The construction of such a grand Buddhist monument would have brought great merit to the king and the concubine. A photograph taken in 1910 shows it in a state of disrepair; it finally collapsed in 1924, as so many people took parts of it home with them as a sign of good luck. A new pagoda was built above the ruins of the old, and opened to the public in 2002. It is now something of a tourist site, brightly lit up at night and forming the backdrop for photographs of visiting dignitaries from all over the world.

'Our meeting on the ferry was destined to happen. I hope you have some affection for me and that you will marry me'. When Xuxuan admitted his poverty, she replied, 'A problem like that is easily solved'. She asked her maid to fetch a parcel wrapped in white cloth, which turned out to contain fifty pieces of silver.

Xuxuan went back to his sister's with the silver, but when his brother-in-law examined the silver carefully, he cried aloud that it had the official seal on it and that it was taken from the municipal treasury. He ran to the treasury and when they tried to trace the Woman in White, they could not find her, but the house she lived in had been long deserted and the neighbours said that it was haunted.

Xuxuan got off the punishment due but was banished from Hangzhou. He went to live in Suzhou, away from his sister. In Suzhou the Woman in White made her appearance and she so charmed his

The Leifeng Pagoda on Sunset Hill, by the West Lake in Hangzhou.

landlord and his family that they were keen for them to get married. The Woman in White was so eager and persuasive that he married her and greatly enjoyed living with her.

One day there was a festival at the Temple of the Golden Mountain, and Xuxuan wished to go and join the fun. His wife was not keen, but assented provided that he promised to not enter the Abbot's dwelling, speak to no monk, and return early to her. To all this Xuxuan readily agreed, but when he arrived at the temple, Fahai the monk came out of the Abbot's lodgings and pursued him to the tempestuous river. Just then a boat appeared, flying through the tempest, and in it were the Woman in White and her maid in blue. At that moment, the monk called out, 'What are you monsters doing here?'. Everyone turned to look at Fahai and the Woman in White, seeing him, rolled the boat over, and went with her maid

A Qing-dynasty ivory snuff bottle depicting
the Woman in White in a boat with her maid.

The Woman in White transforms into a snake; Xuxuan and the monk Fahai look on. Qing-dynasty painting from the Long Corridor of the Summer Palace.

beneath the waves. Fahai said to Xuxuan, 'This woman is a monster. Go back to Hangzhou, and if she troubles you again, let me know'.

When Xuxuan arrived at his sister's in Hangzhou, she blamed him for not telling them about his marriage, and said that his wife had arrived. Xuxuan saw the Woman in White and was scared to go near her. He remembered the monk Fahai, but could not find him, and was on the point of jumping into the river. Just then Fahai appeared and gave him his begging bowl to press down over the Woman's head. When Xuxuan found her with her back to him, he pressed the bowl over her head, further and further down he went, ignoring whatever she was saying. Just then the monk appeared and took the bowl, muttering his spells so that when he looked under the bowl, he saw that she had shrunk into a small snake. She said, 'I was a serpent and the wind and rain drove me to take shelter in the

West Lake. I did not expect to meet with Xuxuan, but I fell in love with him. Although I have infringed the laws of nature, no one has been hurt. Please spare me.' Fahai made her bring her maid, who turned out to be a large blue fish. He stowed the pair of them in his bowl and laid it under Leifeng Pagoda, so that they could never leave. The monsters from Chinese folklore, the transformation of humans into snakes and fish, are all subdued by the construction of a Buddhist pagoda, forming an eternal protection for the local people.

~~~~~~

DAOISM AND POPULAR BELIEFS

The transforming monsters in the story of the Woman in White are typical of traditional folklore, which owes much to Daoism. Daoism, or 'The Way', is an ancient mode of thought, peculiar to China. Its followers seek harmony (*Wu wei*), with the natural order of the world, expressed in the opposing but mutually dependent Yin and Yang: the light and dark, the masculine and feminine, the hot and cool (see p. 47). With the advent of the new religion of Buddhism, however, Daoism tried to compete, in part by copying what the new religion introduced, though some Buddhist practices at first seemed to run counter to Chinese traditions. Monasticism, for example, was thought to be contrary to Chinese ideas of filial piety; moreover, monasteries contributed nothing to the state purse. In India, Buddhist monks lived off alms provided by the populace, but in China they were mostly supported by temple lands donated to them. Eventually, however, the Chinese grew used to the large monasteries that existed everywhere, and even copied the Buddhists, developing their own form of monasticism.

In a six-volume work entitled *The Religious Systems of Ancient China*, J. M. M. de Groot, a Dutch sinologist (1854–1942) who studied Daoism in Fukien, Fujian Province, labelled its beliefs 'animistic'. Even things that the western imagination might regard as 'inanimate', such as trees, animals and rocks, might have an essential spirit, or *jing*, within. Over time, as Buddhist and Daoist gods and goddesses

A Qing-dynasty painting of the White Cloud Temple.

became merged, a series of popular beliefs were established, which formed a mythological background to everyday ritual and life. The Daoist pantheon thus became both enormous and local, with a huge variety of gods and myths that varied from province to province and from period to period, and many of whom became attached to Buddhism in China, manifested in popular beliefs.

THE JADE EMPEROR

When Daoism found itself competing with Buddhism, it took the example of the Emperor of China as its model and proclaimed the Jade Emperor the most important god in heaven. The *Sanqing* ('Three Pure Ones'), who up until then had been the principal Daoist deities (see p. 28), were demoted, becoming the Jade Emperor's attendants. The Jade Emperor's ascendancy reflects the consolidation of the imperial hierarchy, showing increasing reverence for imperial status, a reverence already present in the Han dynasty but accentuated during the Tang dynasty and later. As the equivalent of the earthly Emperor of China, the Jade Emperor was all-powerful on earth as well as in heaven.

THE CHENGHUANGSHEN

China's ancient cities were usually surrounded by a wall and a moat, and the patron Chenghuangshen, or City God, guarded these defences. This tutelary deity first appears in writings of the Northern Qi dynasty, which ruled northern China between 550 and 577 CE. By the middle of the Tang dynasty (618–907 CE), however, as cities expanded, spreading beyond their defensive moats, the Chenghuangshen acquired more and more of the functions of the civic official, looking after all matters to do with security, droughts and floods. In this they absorbed some of the responsibilities of the Tudishen, or Local Gods, which had originally protected the crops of a region but by this time had lost their importance. The Local God's shrine usually lay below that of the City God. The Chenghuangshen even had responsibilities with regards to the Underworld. He was regarded as a protector of the souls of the dead, his image carried through the streets in processions with musicians and banner-carriers at *Qingming* and the Feast of Hungry Ghosts to make sure that angry spirits were calmed. By the Song dynasty, his responsibilities had broadened further, and we also see at this time the Tudishen rising in popularity again, assuming responsibility for various components of a city, such as the dwellings, woodland areas and temple lands. By the Ming (1368–1644) and Qing (1644–1912) dynasties the Chenghuangshen had become so identified with the human city official that all their faults – such as corruption and over-bearing – were imputed to the City God.

HOUSEHOLD GODS

A number of everyday rituals in Chinese homes have developed to appease the domestic gods. Every household kept a small picture of Zao Shen, the Stove God, placed, as the name suggests, over the stove or cooking range. By New Year the image would be smoky and dirty, and people would peel it off the wall and put a new one in its place. As the deity who oversaw everything happening in the household, being so near to where the family congregated for its meals, the Stove God could report on what he observed to his superior, who some say is the Supreme God. On the twenty-third or the twenty-fourth day of the last month of the year, the Stove God would endeavour to make his report. A member of the household, however, might give him something sweet and sticky to eat, so that when he tried to open his mouth he failed to articulate or say anything that might cast the family in a bad light, and could only nod his head, so that his superior passed on to the next in line.

The Stove God may have originated as a God of Fire, during a time before people had their own stoves, but still needed fire to cook food. The Stove God (or his predecessor) certainly dates back to before the Han dynasty, even if sources differ as to his precise

A twentieth-century woodblock print of the Stove God.

name and provenance. On the other hand, sacrifices to him appear at a later date, during the Tang dynasty.

The first emperor of the Tang dynasty, Taizong (599–649), was said to have come down with a feverish cold one day and dreamt of many ghosts and demons making a great noise outside his bedroom. Two of his generals, Qin Shubao and Hu Jingde, offered to put on full armour and guard his door. Knowing they were stationed at the entrance to his room, the emperor slept well that night. Yet he was concerned that they stood all night, so he ordered that portraits of them should be painted in full armour, and so the portraits stood

A twentieth-century New Year print of the Door Gods,
Qin Shubao and Hu Jingde, in full armour.

guard on the two sides of the door. Many variations of this legend
offer different names, but paintings of generals in full armour, traditionally bought during the New Year festivities, are pasted on
doors throughout China to protect the inhabitants of the house
from demons.

GODS OF GOOD FORTUNE

The gods of wealth, longevity and happiness are often thought of
together as the *Sanxing* ('Three Stars'). They were first represented in
human form in the Ming dynasty, but they have a much longer history
in Chinese folklore. Their images are often found in Chinese shops
and restaurants in Britain, as part of the daily rituals of people's lives.

Caishen, the God of Wealth, has a different name in different districts of China; the most popular of these is Zhao Gongming. He is usually portrayed as having a black face, and riding on a tiger. The Ming-dynasty novel *Feng Shen Yan Yi* ('Investiture of the Gods'), a book that accounts for many of the popular gods, reveals how Zhao Gongming was apotheosized by Jiang Ziya. Zhao Gongming was fighting on the side of the last Yin emperor, riding a black tiger and hurling pearls which burst like bombshells, when Jiang Ziya made a straw effigy of him and burnt incense in front of the effigy. After twenty days, Jiang shot peachwood arrows into the heart and eyes of the effigy. At that moment, Zhao Gongming, in the enemy's camp, fainted, shouted and died. Subsequently, Jiang Ziya praised

A twentieth-century New Year print of Caishen,
the God of Wealth, riding on a tiger.

Ming-dynasty embroidery of Shouxing, the God of Longevity, depicted as an elderly man with a domed head. Here he is shown riding a crane and studying a scroll.

Zhao Gongming's bravery to the God of the Underworld and had him canonized as the God of Wealth.

The Shou star became the symbol of longevity, and was deified as Shouxing, or the Old Man of the South Pole. He occupied the first of the twenty-eight stellar places that the Chinese used to calculate the calendar. In the Tang dynasty, this star was believed to control the lifespans of mortals. From the Ming dynasty onwards, Shouxing is usually depicted as a smiling, white-haired old man, carrying a staff that is taller than him, to which is variously attached a gourd, a peach or a scroll, all symbols of longevity.

The cult of Fushen, the God of Happiness, is said to have come from the Tang-dynasty official Yang Cheng. The story goes that he was concerned that the Emperor of Liang, Wu Di, was taking away all the young men who were small of stature from his city to serve him at court. Yang Cheng said to the emperor that he had 'short men as citizens, but they were not his slaves'. The emperor listened to this and released the men. For this, Yang Cheng was made the God of

A Ming-dynasty hanging scroll painting of Fu, Lu and Shu:
the Daoist gods of Fortune, Prosperity and Longevity.

Baleful Stars: Taisui

Not all stars were considered benevolent; in fact, Taisui, the 'Grand Duke Jupiter', is the most feared god in the pantheon. He was more powerful than any other star or planet, believed to be of the wood element, in charge of the Five Directions, the master of the seasons, and the head of all pestilences. His name appears as a god to be feared since the Zhou dynasty; Wang Chong (27–97 CE), the great rationalist of the Han, inveighs against the fear of him. In the Yuan dynasty, it first became a state religion, and Taisui has been worshipped ever since to avert calamity.

In the Daoist almanacs, which every Chinese family must have, it is prohibited to raise any buildings or make any effort to 'open up the earth' (*dongtu*) on certain days relating to Taisui, and weddings are also strictly forbidden. The popularly known words 'Who dares to dig on Taisui's head' is in case they should dig out a lump of human flesh, perhaps because when he was born, Taisui was said to look like a lump of formless flesh. Many people still believe in the negative power of Taisui, and it has great influence in places like Taiwan.

Taisui is the planet Jupiter. It was believed to circle the sun over twelve years, while the earth circles the sun once over one year.

Happiness and came to be worshipped all over the country. In retellings of the Yuan and Ming dynasties, the emperor was believed to belong to the earlier Han dynasty, when there was another emperor by the name of Wu Di, but the story remained the same.

THE EIGHT IMMORTALS

Another popular Daoist symbol of good fortune and longevity are the Eight Immortals: Li Tieguai ('Iron Crutch Li'); Han Zhongli; Zhang Guolao ('Old Man Zhang'); Lu Dongbin; He Xiangu ('Holy Sister He'); Lan Caihe; Han Xiangzi; and Cao Guojiu ('Uncle Cao'). They are a mixed bag of characters and there are huge variations in their stories. Like so many Chinese mythical heroes, they are mostly supposed to have been ordinary mortals who, through their amazing Daoist practice, achieve immortality, ascending to heaven flying on phoenixes or magic swords. They are depicted, singly or collectively, on everything from temple walls to teacups, on objects and in artworks throughout Chinese history. The most popular are Iron Crutch Li, Old Man Zhang and Lu Dongbin.

Li Tieguai was a good-looking Daoist, until he left his body to go to the Western Mountain, Huashan, at the summons of Laozi.

A Ming-dynasty painting of Li Tieguai as a beggar with his iron crutch.

A Journey to the East

The Eight Immortals are first found in the Ming-dynasty novel *Ba Xian Chu Chu Dong You Ji* ('The Eight Immortals on their Journey to the East') by Wu Yuantai, which speaks for the influence of novels on the popular imagination. One episode from the novel describes their journey across the sea to attend a great banquet of the Peaches of Immortality. Each Immortal put down something that would float on the water: Li Tieguai threw down his iron crutch and it floated on the water; Lu Dongbin the pipe that he played on; and Old Man Zhang Guolao his mule. It all went well until the son of the Dragon King took a liking to the jade tablet of Lan Caihe, at which a great battle ensued.

He told the disciple who was watching over his body that even if the weather was warm and his body should putrefy, he was not to touch it until the seventh day had passed. But not long after he had left, his disciple received word that his mother was dying, so he quickly cremated his master's body, regardless of the number of days, and went home. When Li Tieguai returned, he could not find his body to enter again, hard as he tried. In the end, he found a beggar who had recently died, and so he entered that body, and had to put up with all the imperfections that the beggar had died with, including having to use a crutch; hence his nickname, 'Iron Crutch Li'. Another source tells us that he received his iron crutch from the Queen Mother of the West. He was not mentioned until the late Song dynasty.

Zhang Guolao ('Old Man Zhang') rode on a mule, sometimes facing its head, sometimes facing its tail. It carried him thousands of miles in a day, and at the end of the day he would blow on it and fold it up like a piece of paper, then put it away until he needed it next. He supposedly lived in the Tang dynasty, around the time of Emperor Xuanzong, but lived the life of a Daoist hermit and refused all summons to court. When he died of old age, his disciples opened up his coffin to find no body.

Lu Dongbin is perhaps the best-known of the Eight Immortals, and the most 'human' of them. He wandered among the population, often handing out medicine or helping people to solve great personal crises in their lives. He had a humorous outlook and frequented the taverns and bars of Chang'an (today Xi'an), and so was a relatable figure for the bourgeoisie all over China. He was also good with his sword. He still exists in proverbs, a popular one being: 'If you set your dog on Lu Dongbin, it means you cannot tell a good-hearted person'. He is said to have lived during the Tang dynasty, but is not mentioned until the Song dynasty. Many plays were written about him during the Yuan dynasty, and he became particularly popular in stories in the Ming dynasty.

AFTER THE MING

Following the fall of the Ming empire came the Qing dynasty, who were not Han Chinese but Manchu invaders from the north. Since they spoke another language, the Qing had no use for the Chinese scribal class. While the Civil Service Examinations continued, members of the Manchu class took priority over those who had passed the examinations, a reversal of the former order. Although much has been published on the literary products of this time, they were all by the literati, for the literati. These include compendia based

嫁女攗飾玩愛人間婚猿筆歌煀夜深廬尚書圖

Late Qing-dynasty illustration of a scene from
the short story 'Fox marries daughter' in *Liaozhai Zhiyi*
('Strange Tales from a Chinese Studio').

on more ancient books, full of intriguing tales now lost to us, and composed in Classical Chinese, such as the *Liaozhai Zhiyi* ('Strange Tales from a Chinese Studio'). This is a wonderful compendium of tales. Some involve the supernatural, such as stories of beautiful and beguiling women who turn out to be fox fairies, luring young scholars away from their studies. Other stories are more like newspaper reports, for example, one where an earthquake so frightened people that they ran out into the street in their underwear. These are a godsend to modern researchers.

Although the literature and arts of China were flourishing during this period, it was all for internal consumption. When the Emperor Qianlong (r. 1735–96) greeted the embassy led by George Macartney from the United Kingdom in 1793, he was not interested in opening up China to international trade, nor was he interested in the wider world beyond China and its tributaries in Southeast Asia. His rejection of the embassy, ostensibly on the grounds that foreigners would not *kowtow* to the Emperor of China, was buttressed by the apparent self-sufficiency of his kingdom.

Yet after the death of Qianlong, the Manchu government started to decline, and the nineteenth century saw China at a very low ebb on the world stage. Politically, the country descended into chaos: the emperor's jurisdiction did not go far. There was only order where a single man, a local lord, was able to wield power. There were brigands in many areas, and this led to insurrections, some of which became outright rebellions, such as the Taiping Revolution (1850–64), which devastated the whole of southern China. The Qing forces eventually won out, but it was a short-lived victory.

Many of the foreigners who had come to China during the nineteenth century were missionaries, who saw the country as both vulnerable and rich in opportunity. China was far enough to the east that the empires of Europe had not already pounced on it; now, they were keen to dissect it. To these western men, there seemed no limit upon the Chinese people's ability to believe what they wanted: there was no head of a church to dictate a doctrine, no ideological reason for the Chinese people to believe in anything other than what they liked. Many Chinese people were still illiterate, and they took their entertainment as well as their knowledge from the plays that were performed at their village festivals by equally illiterate actors.

Especially in the waning light of the Qing dynasty, the people were left to their own devices, and popular beliefs proliferated. More and more gods, of every conceivable hue, were honoured, with local cults being favoured. It was the missionaries like De Groot, interested in the polytheistic nature of the Chinese religion, rituals and charms, who published much material about this 'new' world, as yet unknown to the west.

But the missionaries were not wholly welcomed by the Chinese. Indeed, resentment about foreign influence and Christian missionaries in particular grew among the rural population, culminating in the *Yihetuan* or 'Boxer' movement (1899–1901), so-called by the westerners who saw Chinese martial arts as a form of boxing. Triggered in part by severe drought, the Boxer Rebellion swept across northern China, leaving a trail of violence in its wake and finally converging on Beijing. The soldiers of the Allied Eight Nations (*baguo lianjun*) – America, Austro-Hungary, Britain, France, Germany, Italy, Japan and Russia – invaded China as a result, storming Beijing and ransacking the Forbidden Palace along with many other places belonging to the emperor, who had fled the city. Thus, in spite of their support for the Qing dynasty, the Boxers precipitated the downfall of the Manchus, and paved the way for the Republic of China.

THE REPUBLIC OF CHINA

The Republic of China was declared on 1 January 1912. Having learnt of the west through Japan, China's new military and political leaders were eager to imitate it, and based the new constitution on those of European countries. The campaigning of radical writers and thinkers led to the unseating of Classical Chinese in favour of a new Standard, or 'Simplified', Chinese, which would eventually be adopted as the official language shortly after the Communist Party took over in 1949. This language was based on the Northern Dialect spoken by the majority of the population and employed abbreviations of the ancient Chinese characters in its script. Han Chinese had no difficulty in coping with Standard Chinese, as it was based on what the people knew as the old vernacular. With the advent of computing and the internet, there has been an official romanization of the script and many methods for digitally inputting it have been contrived (see p. 92).

At first, the Republic was a weak state, unable to maintain centralized control over the whole country. The Warlord Era, in which the country was split into different areas with strong men at the helm, lasted from 1918 to 1926. This period eventually came to an end as the Nationalists, formerly the power base of Sun Yat-sen (1866–1925), leader of the 1911 revolution, gradually took over the whole country; but Civil War would continue to wrack the country as the Nationalist and Communist parties fought for ultimate control of China.

If we think of the Communist Party as extremely left-wing, then the Nationalists were extremely right-wing. Under the leadership of Chiang Kai-shek (1887–1975), the Nationalists became even more conservative, taking as their own the gods and local cults that had flourished under the Manchus. It was at this time, while the Nationalists were the dominant power in China, that the people leaned towards the ancient myths. The more radical Communists, meanwhile, following the example of the Russians, attempted to stamp out the old beliefs in favour of the more scientific dogma that was becoming dominant in Europe.

On top of the conflict between the Nationalist and Communist parties, China was invaded by Japan, sparking the Second Sino-Japanese War (1937–1945). During this time the Nationalists retreated to the west of the country, taking over the whole of Sichuan, including most of the universities and schools, while the Communist Party took as its main base the area round Yan'an. There was a brief interlude when the Communists and the Nationalists joined forces to defy the Japanese. The prolonged military engagement with China occupied much of Japan's resources, allowing the Americans to deal their *coup de grâce* of the Second World War: releasing the atomic bomb over Hiroshima and Nagasaki.

The Chinese Civil War came to an end in 1949, when the Nationalists retreated to the island of Taiwan and the Chairman of the Communist Party Mao Zedong (1893–1976) founded the People's Republic of China. Chairman Mao developed a cult of personality that spread across the country. He insisted that the language and thoughts of the ordinary people should act as guidance to the whole country, and thus launched the Cultural Revolution, which lasted from 1966 until his death in 1976. Central to the Cultural Revolution was Mao's declaration of the 'problem' of the 'Four Olds': Old Ideas, Old Culture, Old Habits and Old Customs. The campaign to destroy the 'Four Olds' was enthusiastically spearheaded by the young in schools and universities, known as the Red Guards. Popular religion suffered greatly during this period and many of the ancient temples were totally destroyed. After Mao's death, his successor as leader of the Communist Party, Deng Xiaoping (1904–97), embarked on a programme of cultural restoration and economic reform. Ever since, China has been on an even keel, leading to its present global power and expanded export market.

A 1960s poster of Chairman Mao depicted as the sun while workers cheer below. The caption reads 'Long live Mao Zedong thought!'

Mao and the Cultural Revolution he instituted are gone – along with his insistence that the language and style of the ordinary people should be paramount. The present government is intent on building up the cities, causing the disappearance of the villages. Universal access to education has increased literacy and knowledge among all Chinese. There is renewed interest among the people in their deep history. The stories of the past are no longer told only in the time-honoured fashion, through performances at village festivals and via the oral tradition, but reimagined in a huge variety of artistic forms including television – which has, as in the west, become the main medium of entertainment. The folklorists are once again, after the devastation of the Cultural Revolution, raising their heads, tracing the old stories through the classics of literature and the oral tradition, and rediscovering their ancient settings. We depend on their invaluable work, digging up the folklore of the past, when we attempt to reconstruct the ever-varied ancient, and not so ancient, myths of China.

APPENDIX

~~~~~~~~~~

TEMPLES AND FESTIVALS
IN MODERN CHINA

Of all the wonders of modern-day China, it is usually its temples, with their highly stylized images of gods and goddesses, that provoke the greatest fascination for foreign travellers. Indeed, most temples in China now function primarily as tourist attractions, given the increase in atheism that accompanied the rise of Communism in the country. The equivalent of 'parish churches' have disappeared: their land was too valuable. What has remained are the 'cathedrals', preserved for their architecture and their historic associations. Among these grand structures are: the Wuta ('Five Pagoda') Temple and Sleeping Buddha Temple, both Buddhist temples near Beijing; the White Cloud Temple, China's leading Daoist temple, also near Beijing; and the Niujie Mosque, which serves the huge Hui (Muslim) population of north China.

TEMPLES

It is very difficult to trace the history of a given temple, since there is little mention of them in written records. Temples could be built or sponsored by anybody and, once up and running, were cheap to maintain; all it took to keep a temple open was donations from a few wealthy people. Very many ancient stories were set in dilapidated,

The Wuta Temple in Beijing has five pagodas and was completed in 1473.
The temple contains hundreds of images of Buddha.

disused temples; they were generally regarded by locals as places of ill omen, though outsiders did not view them the same way. During the Second World War, when China was battling against Japan, many schools and universities were evacuated to the western provinces of China and housed in derelict temples.

There is little difference between the architecture of a temple and, say, a palace building in China, for temples were built in the same way as any secular building, according to *fengshui* conventions. Every temple is centred around a courtyard on a north–south axis, with the main hall in the front courtyard, and further courtyards built to the north containing more halls. The rear of the building should be on higher ground and at the front there should be water.

Entering a Chinese temple, you first negotiate your way around a large screen, which may be painted with dragons in flight; these screens are supposed to keep out demons, as are the temple guardians. These guardians, an import from Indian Buddhism, were introduced to Chinese temples during the Ming dynasty. They usually represent the four Celestial Kings (based on Buddhism's Gods of the Four Directions). The King of the East holds a lute, or *pipa*, and represents the 'middle', as a stringed instrument must not be stretched too much or not enough. The King of the South holds a sword, representing the sword of justice. The King of the West has a snake or dragon wound around his wrist to symbolize his power over other deities, including the important dragon deity who ruled over water (see Chapter Six). Finally, the King of the North holds an umbrella to protect against all pollutions. These figures are often very tall, wear full armour, and have grimacing faces – all the better to scare off demons.

A statue of the King of the East, one of the Four Celestial Kings, holding a *pipa*. From a temple in Lushan.

Inside the courtyards are large containers that await the incense sticks of the faithful, who light them before proceeding to the halls. The first courtyard is sometimes flanked by drum and bell towers that tell the time of day: the bells toll and the drums sound every two hours. These are smaller versions of the drum and bell towers found in such cities as Beijing. Both Buddhist and Daoist temples tend to be noisier than Christian churches. There is no need for people to keep their voices down; this is especially true of Daoist temples.

Inside the main hall sits the image of the deity to whom the temple is dedicated, usually a large sculpture, with other images often to the sides, and offerings placed before it in dishes. Surrounding the image are cushions, arranged in rows for monks to kneel on while they chant sutras. The most striking part of the hall is its large and heavy roof with curved edges. The exterior of the roof is usually covered by ceramic tiles, with figures that decorate the ridges, again to guard against demons. The colour can give an indication of the building's function, for instance, only the imperial palaces were allowed yellow for their ceramic tiles. Only temples and palaces have these heavy roofs. One would have thought that the size and weight of these roofs must be unsafe in earthquake-prone China, but brackets known as *dougong* on top of the pillars hold the roof up and allow it to sway when under the impact of earthquakes. These brackets, made by nameless artisans, were perfected over time: they are made entirely of wood, without even an iron nail. They are often painted so that they appear to be decorative, but are essential to the roof's construction.

Chinese temples typically do not have domes or steeples to give height to the structure, but pagodas may reach over ten storeys tall. There are two kinds of pagodas: the burial places of well-known monks, situated behind temples, where tourists do not usually go; and shrines to deities, which stand in courtyards and can be accessed by all. Nowadays, other halls within temples are often devoted to specific deities, and so the pagoda has lost this latter function, which is only found in earlier structures. However, Lama temples – those from Tibetan Buddhism, which were much in vogue during the last dynasty, the Qing (1644–1912) – often have pagodas that are different from traditional Chinese pagodas, with a rounded top rather than the traditional structure built up layer on layer with jutting-out roofs and eaves. The White Dagoba in Beijing is an example of one such Lama temple.

The survival of religion and belief has been different in China, Hong Kong and Taiwan. During Mao's Cultural Revolution (1966–76), temples were destroyed by the Red Guards, but many have since been reconstructed. Some have been converted to other uses, including

A Buddhist temple in Taiwan.

museums, administrative centres or schools. Others have seen a groundswell of support, from both wealthy local donors and government institutions, since religious freedom has been reinstated. On the island of Taiwan, where the rise of Communism did not destabilize old beliefs, there are so many temples that it is difficult to count them: there is thought to be approximately one for every 1,500 residents. These temples act as local community centres as well as religious and pilgrimage sites. In Hong Kong, many temples exist as they did when it was a 'crown colony', when the British did not interfere greatly with local customs. The local customs and festivals of both Taiwan and Hong Kong, far from the influences of Fukien and Guangzhou, can be very different from the rest of the country.

FESTIVALS

Looking at the traditional festival calendar of China, it quickly becomes apparent that it was created by an agrarian society: the main festival happens during the depth of winter, when agriculturalists have downed tools; the next celebrates the coming of the rains; and, finally, the year winds up with the harvest. This calendar, based on the lunar months, was established by the Western Han Emperor Wu (r. 141–87 BCE), although it may be based on the far more ancient Xia calendar. By the Han dynasty, people were sufficiently well-off to celebrate during the quiet season of the agrarian year, when they were not overtaxed with the hard labour of farming and had a surplus with which to celebrate. By the middle of the prosperous and peaceful Tang dynasty, people were taking life at a much more leisurely pace, and built on these earlier traditions, becoming ever more elaborate in their festivities. Most of the festivals of China date back to these early times.

Festivals were (and still are) held in the open space in villages, and gave people a chance to practise their bartering skills and begin great commercial enterprise. They were also a time of great entertainment, with different troupes of actors and storytellers putting on performances wherever they could find an audience. In rural locales, this was a rare opportunity for communities to come together, to celebrate in their shared culture and prosperity.

The Lunar New Year

The most important annual festival – which, as in many other cultures, takes place during the winter – is the Lunar New Year. When the Republic of China replaced the Manchu rule in 1911 it brought the Gregorian calendar to China, bringing the country in line with the empires of Europe. This celebration was known as the Lunar New Year right up until the founding of the People's Republic of China in 1949, which called it the 'Spring Festival'. But however hard the government tried to make the first day of the Gregorian calendar the New Year's holiday, people stuck to the Lunar New Year. The government took notice and decided that it should be a national holiday; nowadays this has been extended to three days, to allow time for those who need to travel to celebrate with their families. Most people take the whole week off or even longer, celebrating right up until *Yuanxiao*, the Lantern Festival (see p. 212).

The actual celebrations begin earlier, when people clean the house of all the detritus of the previous year. An important part of this is replacing the picture of the Stove God (p. 186), who has sat behind the stove all year and is now a rather dirty and stained picture. People will eat *laba* porridge, named for the eighth (*ba*) day of the last month of the year (*la*), the day on which it was tradition-ally eaten during the Qing dynasty. The porridge is made of eight different kinds of beans and fruits – with regional variation – and eating it has become entwined with religious meaning in Buddhism, especially if you share it with those in need, which gives good omens for the following year.

The tradition of *Shousui* ('Watching the Year Pass'), staying up all night and feasting with the whole family, began in the sixth century. People paste auspicious couplets or words in the *Chunlian* ('Spring Words'), usually on gold-flecked paper in red, beside doors, along with cut-outs of auspicious characters or scenes on red paper – this was the beginning of the folk-art of paper-cutting. Many families put up pictures of the Door Gods (p. 187) or Zhong Kui,

A twentieth-century shadow puppet
of the demon-slayer Zhong Kui.

Chinese folk artists perform a dragon dance to celebrate the Chinese New Year on 1 February 2012 in Taiyuan, Shanxi Province.

the demon-slayer, to scare away any evil demons that might be lurking. Fireworks are also used to scare away demons: in fact, the Chinese invented fireworks for this purpose. Some villages stage lion-dances or string lanterns together to represent the many joints of a dragon (and the pearl that is sometimes depicted with writhing dragons, see p. 132).

Finally, this is the time at which red envelopes are shared, a tradition started in the Yuan dynasty. The Lunar New Year marks the date by which all debts must be paid. These gifts were once given as small sums of money, wrapped in red, from the elders of the house to the young ones; nowadays, with the rise of consumerism, more money changes hands, and there are special envelopes printed with all kinds of modern designs.

The Lantern Festival

The next great festival, which could be said to be a continuation of the Lunar New Year, was *Yuanxiao*, the Lantern Festival. This festival originated in the Han dynasty under Emperor Wu, when the lanterns were lit for the first time. Nowadays, lanterns in all shapes and sizes are strung up for people to enjoy. Also important is the eating of *tangyuan* (called *yuanxiao* in northern China), small balls made of glutinous rice flour, filled with a sweet stuffing, which are usually boiled. They are supposed to represent the moon, which is at its roundest for the first time of the year on the fifteenth day of the first month. They also symbolize the reunion of the family – their name being a pun on the roundness of the moon and the Chinese word for reunion, *tuanyuan*.

A lantern parade in Shanghai rings in the Year of the Pig, 2019.

Tomb-Sweeping Day

Tomb-Sweeping Day, or the *Qingming* ('Bright and Clear') Festival, also takes place near the beginning of the year, just before the spring solstice – usually at the beginning of April – when the weather is warm and sunny. This is the time for people to sweep the tombs of their ancestors, and to perform the ritual obeisance, in an expression of Confucian filial piety. In the past, women of the household who had been secluded all year were allowed to go outside to 'tread the green' (*taqing*). Kite-flying and other outdoor activities also take place.

The Dragon Boat Festival

In June comes *Duanwu*, the Dragon Boat Festival, also known as the Festival of the Fifth of the Fifth Month. This was originally a time to appease the Dragons of the Rainclouds, who were essential for the harvest to go according to plan. If the rains do not appear, especially in the south, then there is danger of drought. People race boats that have dragons painted on their prows, in the hope of tempting out the dragons in the sky. Here, the Confucianists have a hand in the celebrations: the poet Qu Yuan, to whom the *Chu Ci* ('Songs of Chu') are attributed, is honoured at this festival. Yuan offended the king with his distrust of the kingdom of Qin (which in the end swallowed all the states at the end of the Zhou dynasty to found the united China), and for this he was banished from the court. He later drowned himself in the Miluo River. The legend of Qu Yuan remained as the poet who was maligned by the king but beloved of the common people.

Some centuries after the death of Qu Yuan, the Confucianists circulated the story of the ghost of Qu Yuan complaining that he could not taste the food that people cast into the water for him because the 'bad dragons' of the deep had snatched it all. Therefore, the dragon boats were instituted to scatter the 'bad dragons'. So the Confucianists managed to superimpose their version of history onto an ancient rite of rain-making. Other myths are associated with the Fifth of the Fifth Month, but the Qu Yuan legend has stuck, and was especially popular during the war against the Japanese, during which Qu Yuan was again trumpeted as the poet of the people. The festival has turned more recently into a joyous occasion, though there remains some vestige of the old beliefs: young children have their foreheads painted with the character *wang* ('king') using realgar (also called 'ruby sulphur'), a highly poisonous compound that acts as a form of antidote to the bites of snakes and insects that can give rise to illness. This reminds people of the dangers of epidemics that can come with warm weather.

The food most associated with this festival are the *zongzi* made from glutinous rice flour wrapped in bamboo leaves, which originated in the Zhou dynasty. More recently, the double pyramid shape of the *zongzi* has been used for sachets made from different colourful silks. Originally these sachets contained aromatic substances to ward off poisonous insects; nowadays they are empty and are worn by children as ornaments.

The Mid-Autumn Festival

Zhongqiu, the Mid-Autumn Festival, also known as the Moon or Mooncake Festival, is celebrated when the moon is at its roundest, on the fifteenth day of the eighth month of the lunar calendar. It is almost as popular as the Lunar New Year and presents another time for families to come together for a meal or to climb hills and admire the moon. People give each other 'mooncakes' as gifts; these

A mooncake. These delicacies are traditionally
eaten during the Mid-Autumn Festival.

represent the round moon and are full of sweetmeats according to
different local delicacies. It is not known when this festival started,
but ancient kings used to make sacrifices to the moon, and by the
Tang dynasty the festival became more important and the subject
of many poems.

Since Qing times, many festivals have been added to the traditional calendar so that people could have a holiday every month.
These holidays were usually set on the day that matched the number
of the month, such as the fifth of the fifth month, or they took place
on the fifteenth of the month, which falls in the middle of a lunar
month of thirty days.

Before the imperial era, which lasted for over two thousand years, China was not unified. It consisted of many city-states, which acted independently and had their own systems of writing. Many of these were based on ancient tribal networks, which glorified their own ancestors by making them the head of a historic dynasty. Few people could read or write, and they depended on the oral tradition, which is notorious for not giving dates or a timeline until the unification of the imperial era. The first emperor of the hated but short-lived Qin dynasty was a first-rate administrator who systematized many things, including the width of barrows or carriages, but it was the Han who endured and carried on this task, and we now rely on the Han because their rule was long and contained many people who still remembered the times before the Imperial era.

Xia c. 2070–1600 BCE
Shang c. 1600–1046 BCE
Zhou 1046–256 BCE
    Western Zhou 1046–771 BCE
    Eastern Zhou 770–256 BCE
        Spring and Autumn 770–476 BCE
        Warring States 476–221 BCE

IMPERIAL DYNASTIES

Qin 221–207 BCE
Han 202 BCE–220 CE
    Western Han 202 BCE–9 CE
    Xin 9–23 CE
    Eastern Han 25–220 CE
Three Kingdoms 220–280 CE
Jin 266–420
Northern and Southern Dynasties 420–589
Sui 581–618
Tang 618–907
Five Dynasties and Ten Kingdoms 907–979
Liao 916–1127
Song 960–1279
Northern Song 960–1127
Southern Song 1127–1279
Yuan 1271–1368
Ming 1368–1644
Qing 1644–1912

REPUBLIC OF CHINA

Republic of China 1911–1949
People's Republic of China 1949–

The sources offered below are restricted to those in English, though many excellent works addressing the Chinese myths and their history are of course available in different languages.

Birrell, Anne. *Chinese Mythology: An Introduction.*
The Johns Hopkins University Press: Baltimore and London (1993).

Bodde, Derk. 'Myths of ancient China', in *Mythologies of the Ancient World* (ed. Samuel Noah Kramer). Anchor Books, Doubleday: New York (1961).

Christie, A. *Chinese Mythology*. Peter Bedrick Books: New York (1983).

Kaltenmark, M. 'Chinese Mythology', in *Asian Mythologies* (ed. Yves Bonnefoy, trans. Wendy Doniger). University of Chicago Press: Chicago and London (1993).

Maspero, Henri (trans. Frank A. Kierman, Jr.). *Taoism and Chinese Religion*. The University of Massachusetts Press: Amherst (1819).

Yang, Lihui and Deming An, with Jessica Anderson Turner. *A Handbook of Chinese Mythology*. Oxford University Press: Oxford and New York (2005).

SOURCES OF ILLUSTRATIONS

a = above, b = below

gar1984/123RF.com **35**; gyn9037/123RF.com **149**; Wangyouwei/123RF.
com **207**; CPA Media Ltd/Alamy Stock Photo **2, 99, 108, 191**; Granger
Historical Picture Archive/Alamy Stock Photo **55**; Lou-Foto/Alamy
Stock Photo **196**; Walters Art Museum, Baltimore, MD **115**; Morning
Glory Publishers, Beijing **43**; Museum für Östasiastische Kunst, Berlin
210; Birmingham Museum of Art **154**; K. Brashier **165**; Bridgeman
Images **193**; Pictures from History/Bridgeman Images **82**; Cleveland
Museum of Art, OH **58, 174**; © Atiger88/Dreamstime.com **212**; ©
Ottovanrooy/Dreamstime.com **205**; Chester Beatty Library, Dublin
81, 91, 132, 180; Kyushu University Library, Fukuoka **175**; Visual China
Group/Getty Images **211**; British Library, London **44, 53, 78, 84, 93,
111, 171**; Trustees of the British Museum, London **150**; J. Paul Getty
Museum, Los Angeles, CA **11**; LACMA, Gift of Mr and Mrs Eric Lidow
87; LACMA, Far Eastern Council Fund (M.8121) **143**; Minneapolis
Institute of Art, MN **45**; Joseph Needham, *Science and Civilisation in
China*, Vol. 3, Cambridge, 1959 **90**; Cooper Hewitt Smithsonian Design
Museum, New York, NY **61**; Metropolitan Museum of Art, New York,
NY **1, 25, 29, 33, 105, 127, 129, 134, 136, 144, 146, 148, 152, 159, 187, 188,
189**; Princeton University Art Museum, Princeton, NJ **70**; National
Museum of Korea, Seoul **71**; Shizhao/2006 **181**; Mantana Boonsatr/
Shutterstock **215**; cowardlion/Shutterstock **155**; HelloRF Zcool/
Shutterstock **204**; Photo Think A/Shutterstock **179**; Collection of the
National Museum of Singapore, National Heritage Board **131**; Chinese
Art Poster Collection, Whitworth University Library, Spokane, WA **201**;
State Hermitage Museum, St Petersburg **13**; National Palace Museum,
Taiwan **12, 21, 48b, 60, 109, 121, 138, 158, 184, 190**; Drazen Tomic **6–7**;
Library of Congress, Washington, D.C. **31, 41, 51, 67, 96, 101, 123, 157**;
Wellcome Collection **77, 83**; E. T. C. Werner, *Myths and Legends of
China with thirty-two illustrations in colour by Chinese Artists*, London,
1922 **38**; C. A. S. Williams, *Outlines of Chinese Symbolism and Art
Motives*, 1919 **14, 28, 48a, 63, 135, 139, 161**